zoom
Deutsch 1

Foundation
Workbook

Oliver Gray

OXFORD

Great Clarendon Street, Oxford OX2 6DP

Oxford University Press is a department of the University of Oxford.

It furthers the University's objective of excellence in research, scholarship, and education by publishing worldwide in
Oxford New York Auckland Cape Town Dar es Salaam Hong Kong Karachi
Kuala Lumpur Madrid Melbourne Mexico City Nairobi New Delhi Shanghai
Taipei Toronto

With offices in
Argentina Austria Brazil Chile Czech Republic France Greece Guatemala
Hungary Italy Japan South Korea Poland Portugal Singapore Switzerland
Thailand Turkey Ukraine Vietnam

Oxford is a registered trade mark of Oxford University Press in the UK and in certain other countries

British Library Cataloguing in Publication Data

Data available

ISBN 978 019 912771 9

10 9 8

Printed in Great Britain by Ashford Colour Press Ltd, Gosport.

Paper used in the production of this book is a natural, recyclable product made from wood grown in sustainable forests. The manufacturing process conforms to the environmental regulations of the country of origin.

Acknowledgements

The author and publisher would like to thank the following people for their help and advice: Michael Spencer (editor), Angelika Libera (language consultant).

Audio recordings by Boris Steinberg at Slomophone Audio Studio, Berlin

The author and publisher would like to thank the following for their permission to reproduce photographs and other copyright material:

Cover: The Ampelmann is a registered trademark of AMPELMANN GmbH Berlin, www.ampelmann.de

P8tl: Jonathan Larsen/Shutterstock; p8tr: INTERFOTO/Alamy; p8m: OUP; p9l: Nikola Spasenoski/Shutterstock; p9m: Kuttelvaserova/Shutterstock; p9m: Morgan Lane Photography/Shutterstock; p9m: Guy Shapira/Shutterstock; p9m: Monkey Business Images/Shutterstock; p9r: @erics/Shutterstock; p12: Map Resources/Shutterstock; p16: OUP; p33: OUP; p61: imagebroker/Alamy; p72: Elena Aliaga/Shutterstock; p73: Santje/Shutterstock; p74: Bob Cheung/Shutterstock; p75m: Romeo Huidu/Shutterstock; p74b: Pavol Kmeto/Shutterstock.

Illustrations by: Matt Ward, Tim Kahane, Matt Latchford, Stefan Chabluk, James Stayte.

Every effort has been made to contact copyright holders of material reproduced in this book. If notified, the publishers will be pleased to rectify any errors or omissions at the earliest opportunity.

Inhalt

Pronunciation

Sound German!

German letters are not always pronounced like English ones, but the good news is that once you have learnt how to pronounce German, you will always get it right. This isn't true for all languages.

Consonants

Many German consonants are pronounced the same way as in English. Here are some examples:

 Consonants / Konsonanten

b	Berlin
d	Deutsch
f	Fisch
h	Haus
k	klein
l	lustig
m	Mutter
n	nein
p	Polen
t	Timo

Now here are those which sound different:

g *g* is never pronounced like the English 'soft g' (as in the words 'George', 'general' and 'age'). It is always 'hard', as in 'ground', 'gap' or 'gun'.

 g / g

grün
Giraffe
Morgen

j *j* is pronounced like the English 'y'.

 j / j

Joghurt
Jahr
jetzt

r *r* is the reason some people call the German language 'guttural'. It's quite a gritty sound and needs practising because no sound in English is quite like it.

 r / r

rot
Rhein
Regen
Trier
tragen

s *s* is pronounced in various ways:
– like an English 'z';

 s / s

sieben
sechs
singen

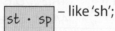 – like 'sh';

 st – sp / st – sp

Straße
Sturm
spielen

s – like an English 's'.

 s / s

lustig
Maske
fast

Berliner Bär

Pronunciation

 v is pronounced like the English 'f'.

 v / v

viel
Vater
vierzig
Vogel
verboten

 w is pronounced like the English 'v'.

w / w

will
Löwe
weiß
Wolke

You can remember *v* and *w* simply by thinking of the word *Volkswagen* (pronounced in the German way, of course).

q and *y* are hardly used at all, so don't worry about them!

'z' is unusual in English (which is why it's worth ten points in Scrabble!). In German, *z* is very common. It is pronounced like the English 'ts'.

z / z

Zoo
Zeit
Zeitung
Zürich

 ß is the only German letter that doesn't exist in the English alphabet. It represents a double *s* when used after a 'long' vowel (see below).

ß / ß

Straße
groß
Fuß

 After a 'short' vowel, *ss* is used instead. It sounds exactly the same.

ss / ss

muss
Schluss
lass
Schloss

Combinations of consonants

 The combination of *c* and *h* sounds similar to the 'ch' at the end of the Scottish word 'Loch'.

ch / ch

acht
Achtung
lachen
Loch

 The 'sh' sound is extremely common in German but it is spelt *sch*.

sch / sch

schade
Fisch
Schule

Achtung! Acht Mädchen lachen!

Pronunciation

Vowels

 The letter *a* can be pronounced as a 'short' vowel or as a 'long' vowel.

The short *a* is pronounced like this:

 Vowels / Vokale
short a / kurzes a

> hat
> machen
> kann
> Mann
> Klasse

> Note that it isn't pronounced exactly like an English 'a' as in when we say 'hat'. It's a little bit like a cross between an 'a' and a 'u', as in the English 'hut'. Listen again to check that.

Long *a* – this sounds like the combination 'ar' in English words like 'car':

 long a / langes a

> Straße
> baden
> haben
> malen

Mmm, Pommes mit Ketchup!

 The short *e* is pronounced like the English 'e', as in 'elephant'. It is never pronounced like the other English 'e', as in 'me'.

 short e / kurzes e

> England
> essen
> frech

There is also a long *e*.

 long e / langes e

> Esel
> sehen
> leben

 The letter *i* is always pronounced short, as in the English 'in'.

 i / i

> in
> Interview
> billig
> ich

 The short *o* is pronounced like this:

 short o / kurzes o

> toll
> doppel
> Pommes

The long *o* is pronounced like this:

 long o / langes o

> Mode
> Cola
> Hallo

Pronunciation

 The short *u* is pronounced like this:

🎧 **short u / kurzes u**

Hund
muss
lustig

The long *u* is pronounced like this:

🎧 **long u / langes u**

Stuhl
Schule
Buch

Combinations of vowels

When two vowels are used together, they make a different sound. This is very common in German.

 ie is pronounced as in the English word 'keep'.

🎧 **ie / ie**

viel
Liebe
sie
vier

 ei is pronounced as in the English word 'eye'.

🎧 **ei / ei**

mein
dein
kein
heiße

 au is pronounced as in the English word 'cow'.

🎧 **au / au**

Haus
Maus
blau

Umlauts

An umlaut is a little symbol that changes the sound of an *a*, *o* or *u*.

Listen to the difference the umlauts make to the sound of each letter.

a · ä

🎧 a ⟶ ä

Vater / Väter
hatte / hätte
Hand / Hände

o · ö

🎧 o ⟶ ö

Post / hören
rot / Löwe
schon / schön

u · ü

🎧 u ⟶ ü

muss / müssen
Gruß / grüßen
pur / für

Eine Maus in einem Haus!

1 🎧 **Listen to some German names being spelled out. Write down the names.**

a __Katja__   g _____ _____

b _____   h _____ _____

c _____   i _____ _____

d _____   j _____ _____

e _____

f _____

2 **How do you say these things in German?**
Write them in and say them out loud.

a Say 'Good morning' to someone.

    _Guten Morgen!_____

b Ask how to write that.

    _____

c Ask what someone's name is.

    _____

d Say 'Good evening' to someone.

    _____

e Say what your name is.

    _____

f Say 'Goodbye'.

    _____

> Auf Wiedersehen!   Wie heißt du?   Guten Abend!
> Ich heiße …   Wie schreibt man das?   Guten Morgen!

3 **Say these English words out loud. What German letters do they represent?**

a HA! ____   d SAY ____

b BAY ____   e YACHT ____

c CAR ____   f DAY ____

1 🎧 **Listen to these people giving you their ages. Write the ages in the bubbles.**

a 18   b   c   d   e   f

2 **Add the prices to the labels.**

a 2,00 €

b

c

d

e

f

Hamburger – drei Euro zehn

Schokolade – zwei Euro zwanzig

Bananen – zwei Euro

CD – sechzehn Euro fünfzehn

Lampe – vierzehn Euro

Cola – ein Euro fünfzehn

3 **These people are giving their ages. Write down what they are saying.**

a Ich bin elf Jahre alt.

b _____

c _____

d _____

e _____

f _____

a 11   b 17   c 9   d 19   e 7   f 20

zwanzig   neun   neunzehn   sieben   siebzehn   elf

1 Solve the clues and write in the German names of the months. The highlighted letters spell another month.

a The seventh month of the year.
b A month for Valentines.
c The month before the month in clue **a**.
d The month after the month in clue **a**!
e It sounds like 'my'.
f A month with a 'Fool's Day'.

Februar   April   Mai
Juni   Juli   August

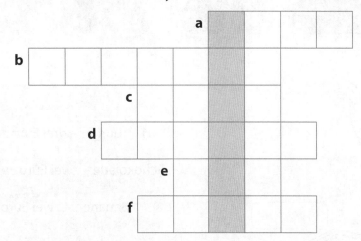

2 Do the sums, then write the answers, first the number, then the German word. Some words will be left over.

a 3 x 7 =   ___21___   ___einundzwanzig___

b 2 x 15 = _____   _____

c 12 + 12 = _____   _____

d 15 + 12 = _____   _____

e 31 – 9 = _____   _____

f 24 + 4 = _____   _____

einundzwanzig   zweiundzwanzig   dreiundzwanzig
vierundzwanzig   fünfundzwanzig   sechsundzwanzig
siebenundzwanzig   achtundzwanzig
neunundzwanzig   dreißig   einunddreißig

3 Listen and work out how old these people are.

a ___21___   c _____   e _____

b _____   d _____   f _____

1 Find the names of eight countries in this grid. The words can be horizontal, vertical or diagonal.

Deutschland
Frankreich
Großbritannien
Österreich
Polen
Schweiz
Spanien
Türkei

G	R	O	B	R	T	N	N	E	N	D	U	E	T
ß	R	Ä	D	E	U	T	S	C	H	L	A	N	D
Ö	P	O	L	E	N	Ü	M	C	O	P	O	L	R
K	N	R	ß	V	B	R	I	F	S	V	U	T	S
A	R	Ä	K	B	F	E	ß	G	T	F	R	K	S
G	B	R	I	T	R	Z	F	B	E	N	G	L	A
ß	P	C	O	R	A	I	Z	F	R	W	S	M	R
A	L	L	E	G	N	D	T	J	R	V	C	I	S
D	E	T	Z	D	K	ß	L	A	E	E	H	Z	P
E	S	Ü	Ü	B	R	V	A	L	N	D	W	Ü	A
Ö	M	R	P	K	E	F	M	S	I	N	E	R	N
S	E	K	R	M	I	L	D	H	S	T	I	C	I
E	B	E	Ä	H	C	H	S	H	C	H	Z	E	E
T	Ü	I	R	K	H	Ö	G	F	H	A	B	H	N

2 Unjumble the countries and insert the language.

a Ich komme aus (tslDhcuaend) _Deutschland_ . Ich spreche _____ .

b Ich komme aus (seÖrictreh) _____ .

Ich spreche _____ .

c Ich komme aus (khainecrrF) _____ .

Ich spreche _____ .

d Ich komme aus (lenoP) _____ . Ich spreche _____ .

e Ich komme aus (pieSnan) _____ .

Ich spreche _____ .

f Ich komme aus (rnßenobiritanG) _____ .

Ich spreche _____ .

3 Fill in the gaps with information about yourself.

Ich heiße _____ . Ich komme aus _____ .

Ich bin _____ Jahre alt. Ich habe im _____ Geburtstag.

Ich spreche _____ .

1 Complete these sentences to show what Nüssi the squirrel thinks of the seasons. The information is given below in English.

a Dezember ist _schlecht_ .

b März ist _____ .

c Juni ist _____ .

d Juli ist _____ .

e August ist _____ .

f Oktober ist _____ .

gut	super
sehr gut	fantastisch
nicht gut	schlecht

Nüssi the squirrel thinks October isn't good.
She thinks July is fantastic but December is bad.
June is super, August is good and March is very good.

2 When are these people's birthdays? Write down the month in English.

a _January_

b _____

c _____

d _____

e _____

f _____

3 Say the month of each person's birthday.

Wann hast du Geburtstag?

Ich habe im Juni Geburtstag.

22.06.	14.03.	03.08.
12.07.	26.11.	04.12.

1 Put these words into the correct column.

Country	Language
Italien	Italienisch

One of the countries has three languages. Put that one last.

Italien   Englisch   Spanien   Türkei   Polen
Deutsch   Polnisch   Italienisch   Schweiz   Deutschland
Französisch   Frankreich   Großbritannien   Türkisch   Spanisch

2 Using your knowledge of German pronunciation, say these German words out loud. Then check the recording to see how accurate you were.

ich   Wien   zwei   zwölf   schlecht
dreißig   Frankreich   Tschüs   wie
Griechenland   fünf

3 Insert the correct form of *haben* (to have) or *sein* (to be).

a Wann ___hast___ du Geburtstag?

b Ich _____ im Dezember Geburtstag.

c Wie alt _____ du?

d Ich _____ 12 Jahre alt.

e _____ du im Januar Geburtstag?

f Nein, ich _____ im Dezember Geburtstag!

habe   hast   habe   Hast   bin   bist

Numbers in German

German numbers over 20 are different from English numbers because the second number comes first. For example, 'twenty-three' is *dreiundzwanzig*, so the first thing you hear is the three.

Be aware of this when you are asking about important numbers such as train times, telephone numbers etc. Try to get in the habit of noting the second number first, so you don't end up missing your train.

1   Take it in turns to say numbers between twenty and thirty to a partner. If you want to hear them again, say '*Wie, bitte?*'.

ei and *ie*

The pronunciation and spelling of *ei* and *ie* is probably the most common error made by learners of German.

Look at the pictures: *ei* is pronounced like the English word 'eye'; *ie* is pronounced 'eee'. Keep them in mind when listening to and speaking German.

EI   **IE**

2   Read these words aloud and get a partner to write them down accurately:

Wien	zwei	drei	wie	dreißig	Frankreich	zweiunddreißig
viel	Griechenland	mein	sieben	heißt	vier	

Keeping a vocabulary list

It's a good idea to have a notebook with a separate page for each letter of the alphabet where you can jot down any new words you come across. Remember to note the gender of each noun (*der, die, das*) and to put a capital letter on each. If you have room, you could also keep verbs, nouns, adjectives and adverbs separate.

Learning vocabulary

There are lots of different ways to learn vocabulary. Try some of these out and see which works best for you:
- make a mind map of all the words which relate to a particular topic
- draw pictures next to words in your vocabulary list to help you remember them
- make connections with similar words in English, e.g. *elf* (11) and 'elf'.

1 bis 31	**1 to 31**
eins, zwei, drei	*one, two, three*
vier, fünf, sechs	*four, five, six*
sieben, acht, neun	*seven, eight, nine*
zehn, elf, zwölf	*ten, eleven, twelve*
dreizehn	*thirteen*
vierzehn	*fourteen*
fünfzehn	*fifteen*
sechzehn	*sixteen*
siebzehn	*seventeen*
achtzehn	*eighteen*
neunzehn	*nineteen*
zwanzig	*twenty*
einundzwanzig	*twenty-one*
zweiundzwanzig	*twenty-two*
dreiundzwanzig	*twenty-three*
vierundzwanzig	*twenty-four*
fünfundzwanzig	*twenty-five*
sechsundzwanzig	*twenty-six*
siebenundzwanzig	*twenty-seven*
achtundzwanzig	*twenty-eight*
neunundzwanzig	*twenty-nine*
dreißig	*thirty*
einunddreißig	*thirty-one*

Wie alt bist du?	**How old are you?**
Ich bin … Jahre alt.	*I am … years old.*
Ich habe am … Geburtstag.	*My birthday is on the …*
Ich habe im … Geburtstag.	*My birthday is in …*
Wann hast du Geburtstag?	*When is your birthday?*
am ersten/zweiten/dritten/ vierten	*on the first/second/third/fourth*
am zwanzigsten	*on the twentieth*

Monate	**Months**
Januar	*January*
Februar	*February*
März	*March*
April	*April*
Mai	*May*
Juni	*June*
Juli	*July*
August	*August*
September	*September*
Oktober	*October*
November	*November*
Dezember	*December*

Wie geht's?	**How are you?**
Mir geht's gut	*I feel good, I'm well*
sehr gut	*very good*
fantastisch	*fantastic*
nicht so gut	*not so good*
schlecht	*bad*

Hallo	**Hello**
Guten Tag	*Hello/Good day*
Guten Morgen	*Good morning*
Guten Abend	*Good evening*
Auf Wiedersehen	*Goodbye*
Tschüs	*Bye*

Wie heißt du?	**What's your name?**
Ich heiße …	*My name is/I am called …*
Wie schreibt man das?	*How do you spell that?*
Das schreibt man …	*That is spelled …*

Länder	**Countries**
Ich komme aus …	*I come from … (+ country)*
Ich wohne in …	*I live in … (+ country)*
Deutschland	*Germany*
die Schweiz	*Switzerland*
die Türkei	*Turkey*
Frankreich	*France*
Österreich	*Austria*
Polen	*Poland*
Spanien	*Spain*

Sprachen	**Languages**
Ich spreche …	*I speak … (+ language)*
Deutsch	*German*
Englisch	*English*
Französisch	*French*
Italienisch	*Italian*
Spanisch	*Spanish*

Checklist

How well do you think you can do the following? Write a sentence for each one if you can.	I can do this well	I can do this but not very well	I can't do this yet
1 say your name, age and when your birthday is			
2 use the German alphabet			
3 pronounce the letters *ä, ö, ü, ß, w* and *ch* correctly			
4 count from 1–31			
5 use the verbs *haben* and *sein* in the *ich* and *du* forms			
6 name a few countries and languages			

1A.1 Das ist meine Familie!

1 Emine is introducing her family. Fill in the gaps with a name.

Ich heiße Emine. Das ist meine Familie.

Mehmet

Suzan

Hassan

Rafat

Ayse   Ahmed

a _____Mehmet_____ ist mein Vater.

b _____ ist meine Mutter.

c _____ ist meine Schwester.

d _____ ist mein Bruder.

e _____ ist mein Opa.

f _____ ist meine Oma.

2 🎧 Listen to Sascha describing his family. Who is who?

Father: _____Boris_____

Mother: _____

Sister: _____

Brother: _____

Klaus   Maria   Susanne   Boris

3 Add in an *–e* if required. If it's not required, leave it blank.

mein___ Bruder

mein___ Schwester

mein___ Oma

mein___ Vater

mein___ Opa

mein___ Großeltern

mein___ Mutter

1 **Match the sentences to the pictures.**

1

3

5

2

4

6

a [6] Ich habe zwei Schwestern.

b [ ] Ich habe einen Bruder.

c [ ] Ich habe eine Schwester.

d [ ] Ich habe zwei Brüder.

e [ ] Ich bin Einzelkind.

f [ ] Ich habe eine Schwester und einen Bruder.

2 🎧 **Listen to these people (a–f). How many brothers and sisters do they have?**

a ___no___ brother(s)   ___two___ sister(s)

b _____ brother(s)   _____ sister(s)

c _____ brother(s)   _____ sister(s)

d _____ brother(s)   _____ sister(s)

e _____ brother(s)   _____ sister(s)

f _____ brother(s)   _____ sister(s)

3 **Translate these sentences.**

a I've got two brothers.   Ich habe ___zwei___ ___Brüder___.

b I've got one sister.   Ich habe _____ _____.

c I've got two sisters.   Ich habe _____ _____.

d I've got one brother.   Ich habe _____ _____.

e I've got three brothers.   Ich habe _____ _____.

f I've got no brothers or sisters.   Ich habe _____ _____.

1 Colour in these animals correctly.

a

c

e

b

d

f

Das ist ein Hund. Er ist schwarz.
Das ist eine Maus. Sie ist weiß.
Das ist ein Wellensittich. Er ist gelb.

Das ist eine Katze. Sie ist braun und weiß.
Das ist eine Schildkröte. Sie ist grau.
Das ist ein Pferd. Es ist braun.

2 🎧 Listen to these people. What pets do they have? Write the answers in English.

a _two cats_____

b _____

c _____

d _____

e _____

f _____

3 Decide whether these words are singular or plural.

a Mäuse   singular / (plural)

b Pferde   singular / plural

c Wellensittich   singular / plural

d Fisch   singular / plural

e Hühner   singular / plural

f Hunde   singular / plural

1 Write in the adjectives. What is the mystery word down?

The mystery word down is _____. It means _____.

2 🎧 Kalle Klug is a cool guy. Which adjectives apply to him?

a schüchtern   ja / (nein)

b intelligent   ja / nein

c sportlich   ja / nein

d klein   ja / nein

e groß   ja / nein

f musikalisch   ja / nein

1 🎧 **Listen and answer these questions in English.**

Hi! Ich heiße Tim.

a How old is Tim?

Tim is _____

b Where does he live?

_____

c How old is his sister?

_____

d What is she like? Mention two characteristics.

_____

e How old is Tim's brother?

_____

f What is he like? Mention two characteristics.

_____

2 **Unjumble the words to make animals. Write out the German word and its English translation.**

a E N F L I D   Delfin _____ , dolphin _____

b F A F E   _____ , _____

c H A S N O N R   _____ , _____

d W Ö L E   _____ , _____

e G O L E V   _____ , _____

f F E N E L A T   _____ , _____

3 **Write down these animals and their characteristics in English.**

a Ein Delfin ist sportlich, intelligent und fleißig.
b Ein Löwe ist laut, faul und frech.

a _____

b _____

Gender

All nouns are masculine, feminine or neuter:

masculine	ein Fisch	er
feminine	eine Maus	sie
neuter	ein Kaninchen	es

Possessive adjectives

	masculine	feminine	neuter
my	mein Bruder	meine Schwester	mein Pferd
your	dein Onkel	deine Tante	dein Meerschweinchen

Example:

sister, Paula

1 **Write full sentences like the example provided.**

Example: _Das ist meine Schwester. Sie heißt Paula._

a _____

b _____

c _____

d _____

e _____

f _____

a
brother, Klaus

d
aunt, sporty

e
brown

b
granddad, Helmut

f
parents

c
Schnurri

Negative

masculine	Ich habe keinen Hamster.
feminine	Ich habe keine Schwester.
neuter	Ich habe kein Meerschweinchen.

2 **Complete the sentence using _kein_ or _keine_.**

Ich habe keinen_____ H_____, k_____ K_____,

k_____ P_____ und k_____ G_____ .

Umlauts

1 Say these words out loud.
Get a partner to assess how well you have pronounced them.

> **u / ü:** Hund – schüchtern – Mutter – Mütter – grün – müde
> **o / ö:** Opa – Schildkröte – Onkel – Löwe – schon – schön – zwölf – Oma
> **a / ä:** Nashorn – Bär – Vater – Väter – Apfel – Äpfel – Affe

An 'umlaut' is an item of punctuation found in German but not in English. It changes how a vowel is pronounced. Umlauts are only used with u, o and a.

Noun or adjective?

2 Decide whether these words are nouns or adjectives.
Write them in the correct column.

Noun	Adjective
Affe	

> AFFE
> TIGER
> NETT
> SCHWESTER
> BLAU
> ROMANTISCH
> SCHWARZ
> OPA
> SCHLANGE
> FAUL
> EINZELKIND
> GRÜN

Nouns are usually easy to identify in German, as they all start with a capital letter, but here it is more difficult, as the words are printed in capitals.

Singular or plural?

3 Use the vocabulary page to work out the plural of these nouns.

Hund, Mutter, Giraffe, Schlange, Bruder, Katze, Papagei, Schwester, Vater

Hunde,

In English, we mainly make a noun plural by adding an –s. It's very different in German, where there are different ways of making plurals.

Dictionary skills

4 Look up these nouns, which you may not know. Write down the meaning and show you understand the gender by writing *der*, *die* or *das*.

das Geld money   ___ Arbeit ___
___ Polizei ___   ___ Auto ___
___ Tür ___   ___ Fenster ___
___ Boot ___   ___ Wald ___

When looking up a noun, the dictionary will tell you whether it is masculine (m), feminine (f) or neuter (n).

5 Find the infinitive and the meaning of these new verbs in the dictionary.

ich laufe laufen , to run   wir bleiben ___ , ___

er bringt ___ , ___   ich lerne ___ , ___

When looking up a verb, the dictionary will show you the infinitive form.

Meine Familie — *My family*

Wer ist das?	*Who's that?*
Ist das dein/e (Vater/Mutter)?	*Is that your (father/mother)?*
Sind das deine (Großeltern)?	*Are these your (grandparents)?*
Hast du Geschwister?	*Do you have siblings?*
Das ist mein/e (Bruder/ Schwester).	*This is my (brother/sister).*
Das sind (meine Brüder).	*These are (my brothers).*
Ja, ich habe (einen Bruder).	*Yes, I have (a brother).*
Nein, ich bin Einzelkind.	*No, I'm an only child.*
Er/sie heißt (Jens/Julia).	*He/she is called (Jens/Julia).*
ein Bruder(-üder)	*a brother*
ein Onkel(-)	*an uncle*
ein Opa(-s)	*a granddad*
ein Vater(-äter)	*a father*
eine Familie(-n)	*a family*
eine Mutter(-ütter)	*a mother*
eine Oma(-s)	*a grandmother*
eine Schwester(-n)	*a sister*
eine Tante(-n)	*an aunt*
Eltern	*parents*
Großeltern	*grandparents*

Haustiere — *Pets*

ein Fisch(-e)	*a fish*
ein Hamster(-)	*a hamster*
ein Huhn(-ühner)	*a chicken*
ein Hund(-e)	*a dog*
ein Kaninchen(-)	*a rabbit*
eine Katze(-n)	*a cat*
eine Maus(-äuse)	*a mouse*
ein Meerschweinchen(-)	*a guinea pig*
ein Pferd(-e)	*a horse*
eine Schildkröte(-n)	*a tortoise*
eine Schlange(-n)	*a snake*
ein Wellensittich(-e)	*a budgie*

Tiere im Zoo — *Zoo animals*

ein Affe(-n)	*a monkey*
ein Bär(-en)	*a bear*
ein Delfin(-e)	*a dolphin*
ein Elefant(-en)	*an elephant*
eine Giraffe(-n)	*a giraffe*
ein Löwe(-n)	*a lion*
ein Nashorn(-örner)	*a rhino*
ein Papagei(-en)	*a parrot*
ein Tiger(-)	*a tiger*
ein Vogel(-ögel)	*a bird*

Wie bist du? — *What are you like?*

faul	*lazy*
fleißig	*hard-working*
frech	*naughty*
groß	*tall, big*
intelligent	*intelligent*
klein	*small*
laut	*loud*
musikalisch	*musical*
nett	*nice*
romantisch	*romantic*
schüchtern	*shy*
sportlich	*sporty*
gar nicht	*not at all*
nicht	*not*
ziemlich	*quite*
sehr	*very*

Farben — *Colours*

blau	*blue*
braun	*brown*
gelb	*yellow*
grau	*grey*
grün	*green*
orange	*orange*
rot	*red*
schwarz	*black*
weiß	*white*

Checklist

How well do you think you can do the following?

Write a sentence for each one if you can.

	I can do this well	I can do this but not very well	I can't do this yet
1 talk about your family			
2 use the words for 'my' and 'your'			
3 use *Ich habe eine(n)/ keine(n)* …			
4 use plurals			
5 describe yourself, friends, family and pets			
6 use *er/sie/es* correctly			

1B.1 Mein Klassenzimmer

1 Fill the gaps with a question word or article from the box below.

a

b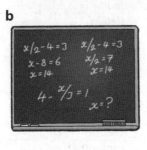

c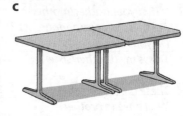

d

a __Wer__ ist das? Das ist _____ Schülerin.

b _____ ist das? Das ist _____ Tafel.

c _____ ist das? Das ist _____ Schreibtisch.

d _____ ist das? Das ist _____ Lehrer.

e _____ ist das? Das ist _____ Schüler.

f _____ ist das? Das ist _____ Stuhl.

e

f

> Wer   Was   der   die   das

2 🎧 What do these people have? Put a tick or a cross.

a Katja: ✓ ☐

b Sven: ☐   ☐

c Kim: ☐   ☐

d Fabian: ☐   ☐

1 Fill in the crossword with school subjects.

Waagerecht (across)

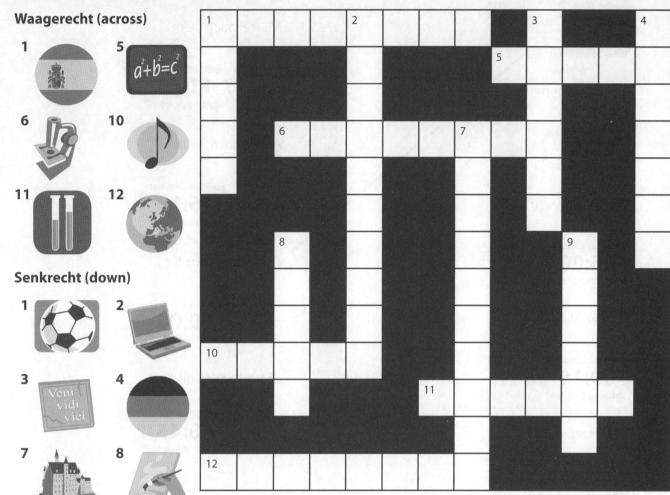

Senkrecht (down)

2 🎧 Listen and decide what these people think of the subjects. Answer in English.

a Janina thinks Spanish is _____super_____ but French is _____ .

b Karl thinks ICT is _____ and maths is _____ .

c Nicole thinks art is _____ but geography is _____ .

d Nils thinks English is _____ but sport is _____ .

1 Draw lines to link the times to the clocks.

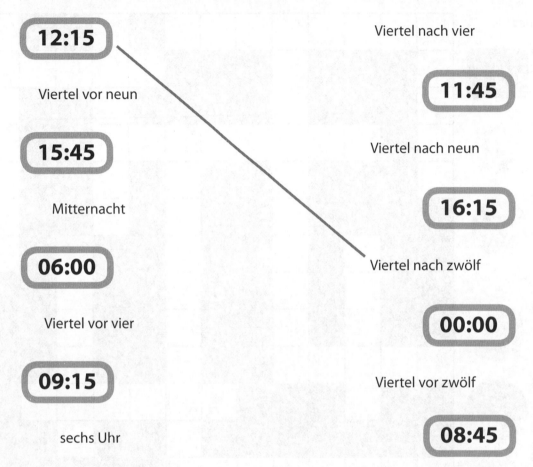

12:15

Viertel nach vier

Viertel vor neun

11:45

15:45

Viertel nach neun

Mitternacht

16:15

06:00

Viertel nach zwölf

Viertel vor vier

00:00

09:15

Viertel vor zwölf

sechs Uhr

08:45

2 🎧 Listen and fill in the gaps in the timetable to show when each lesson starts.

	Time	Subject
1	8.15	art
2		maths
3		English
4		French
5		ICT
6		sport

1 Find the German words for the days of the week in this grid (across, down or diagonally).

M	I	S	A	M	S	T	A	G	S	O	N
D	O	N	N	I	N	G	S	A	M	P	R
O	R	N	A	T	A	G	O	L	L	A	H
N	M	O	P	T	R	S	T	U	Z	L	A
N	E	I	N	W	D	W	O	C	H	G	N
E	I	N	M	O	N	T	A	G	A	M	D
R	O	T	A	C	H	T	U	T	N	G	S
S	F	R	I	H	E	D	I	A	H	C	O
T	Z	W	E	D	I	E	N	S	T	A	G
A	G	A	S	T	R	F	W	C	H	O	M
G	R	E	A	F	E	I	R	A	G	T	S

Montag

Dienstag

Mittwoch

Donnerstag

Freitag

Samstag

Sonntag

2 Unjumble these sentences to say what subjects these people have on which day.

a ich Donnerstag Musik Am Mathe habe und

   Am Donnerstag habe ich Musik und Mathe.

b Erdkunde Spanisch und Montag ich Am habe

c habe und Kunst Am ich Biologie Freitag

d Am Latein Englisch und ich Dienstag habe

e Mittwoch ich Informatik Am habe Deutsch und

1 Fill in this timetable in German for Monday, Tuesday and Wednesday. There may be some double lessons.

	Montag	Dienstag	Mittwoch	Donnerstag	Freitag
08.45	Religion				
10.00					
10.45					
11.30					
12.15					
13.00					

Monday, 10.45: art

Tuesday, 11.30: German

Monday, 08.45: religion

Tuesday, 13.00: French

Monday, 11.30: biology

Tuesday, 8.45: maths

Wednesday, 12.15: English

Tuesday, 10.45: geography

Wednesday, 13.00: English

Wednesday, 08.45: Italian

Monday, 13.00: sport

Wednesday, 10.00 Italian

Monday, 12.15: Spanish

Wednesday, 11.30: French

Monday, 10.00: history

Wednesday, 10.45: chemistry

Tuesday, 10.00: maths

Tuesday 12.15: ICT

2 🎧 Now listen and fill in the lessons for Thursday and Friday.

Geschichte	Chemie	Musik
Kunst	Französisch	Mathe
Biologie	Englisch	Latein
Spanisch	Informatik	Religion
Erdkunde	Deutsch	Sport
Italienisch	Physik	

Articles

1 Write in the correct word for 'the' for these words. The gender is given in brackets.

<u>der</u> Stuhl (m)   _____ Schreibtisch (m)   _____ Klassenzimmer (n)

_____ Lehrer (m)   _____ Lehrerin (f)   _____ Tafel (f)

_____ Heft (n)   _____ Schülerin (f)   _____ Schüler (m)

_____ Direktor (m)   _____ Bibliothek (f)   _____ Schulhof (m)

> m = masculine = der
> f = feminine = die
> n = neuter = das

haben

2 Use the correct form of *haben* in these sentences.

a Am Montag ___<u>habe</u>___ ich Mathe.

b Am Freitag _____ er Spanisch.

c Am Dienstag _____ wir Kunst.

d Am Mittwoch _____ du Informatik.

e Am Donnerstag _____ wir Physik.

f Am Montag _____ ich Sport.

> ich habe
> du hast
> er/sie/es hat
> wir haben

Word order

3 Write sentences based on the clues. Use the *wir* form.

a Tuesday <u>Am Dienstag haben wir Mathe.</u>

> Remember, the verb comes second.

b Monday _____

c Friday _____

d Wednesday _____

e Thursday _____

> Montag
> Dienstag
> Mittwoch
> Donnerstag
> Freitag
> Kunst
> Deutsch
> Informatik
> Musik

Recognising words

1 Use the clues to help you find the words.
Write the words in English and German.

For the activities on this page, refer to the vocabulary page of your text book.

Clue	English word	German word
a A 'pocket reckoner'	calculator	Taschenrechner
b Something to keep papers in **order**	_____	_____
c Something you sit at when you **write**	_____	_____
d Something you **fill** with ink	_____	_____
e A subject concerning the **earth**	_____	_____
f Like a **stool** but with a back on it	_____	_____
g In the **middle** of the **night**	_____	_____
h In the **middle** of the **week**	_____	_____
i A subject that gives you **information**	_____	_____
j Something used for drawing **lines**	_____	_____

Ordner   Mittwoch   Lineal   Stuhl   Taschenrechner

Erdkunde   Mitternacht   Informatik   Füller   Schreibtisch

German is a good language for guessing the meanings of words because it is a logical language and often combines two or more words into one. In the first example, *Tasche* means 'pocket' and *Rechner* means 'reckoner'. A 'pocket reckoner' is a calculator. With a bit of logical thought and clever guess work, there are lots of words you can understand.

Similar words

2 **Circle any word that you can immediately recognise because it is so similar to an English word. If there are any borderline cases, discuss them with others in the class.**

Englisch   Deutsch   Stuhl   fantastisch   langweilig

interessant   Kunst   Latein   super   Dienstag   Spanisch

Lieblingsfach   Sport   doof   Mathe   Musik

You can get off to a good start in understanding German because so many words are similar to English ones.

Ways to pronounce 'o'

3 **These are all words you have come across in this unit. Can you remember how to pronounce them? Say them out loud.**

doof   Ordner   Montag   Sport

Sonntag   Nashorn   Religion   Wolf

This one vowel can be pronounced in various ways.

1B Vokabular

Mein Klassenzimmer	**My classroom**
das Klassenzimmer	classroom
der Lehrer	teacher (male)
die Lehrerin	teacher (female)
der Schreibtisch	desk
der Schüler	pupil (male)
die Schülerin	pupil (female)
der Stuhl	chair
die Tafel	board, chalkboard

Schulsachen	**School equipment**
der Bleistift	pencil
die Federtasche	pencil case
der Filzstift	felt-tip pen
der Füller	fountain pen
das Heft	exercise book
der Kuli	ballpoint pen
das Lineal	ruler
der Ordner	file
der Radiergummi	eraser
das Schulbuch	school book
die Schultasche	school bag
der Taschenrechner	calculator

Schulfächer	**School subjects**
Deutsch	German
Englisch	English
Erdkunde	geography
Französisch	French
Geschichte	history
Informatik	IT
Kochen	cookery
Kunst	art
Latein	Latin
Mathe	maths
Medienwissenschaften	media studies
Naturwissenschaften (Biologie, Chemie, Physik)	sciences (biology, chemistry, physics)
Religion	religion, RE
Spanisch	Spanish
Sport	PE
Turnen	gymnastics

Meinungen	**Opinions**
Wie findest du (Mathe)?	What do you think of (maths)?
Ich finde (Mathe) toll.	I think (maths) is great.
Ich finde (Mathe) nicht toll.	I don't think (maths) is great.
Magst du (Kunst)?	Do you like (art)?
Ich mag (Kunst).	I like (art).
Ich mag (Kunst) nicht.	I don't like (art).
Was ist dein Lieblingsfach?	What's your favourite subject?
Mein Lieblingsfach ist (Sport).	My favourite subject is (sport).
einfach	easy

interessant	interesting
fantastisch	fantastic
furchtbar	awful
gut	good
langweilig	boring
prima	fabulous
doof	stupid
schwer	difficult
super	super

Wie spät ist es?	**What time is it?**
Es ist …	It is …
neun Uhr	nine o'clock
halb neun	half past eight
Viertel vor neun	quarter to nine
Viertel nach neun	quarter past nine
Mittag	12 o'clock (noon)
Mitternacht	12 o'clock (midnight)

Wann haben wir Mathe?	**When do we have maths?**
Um wie viel Uhr beginnt Kunst?	At what time does art begin?
Wir haben um zehn Uhr Mathe.	We have maths at ten o'clock.
Kunst beginnt um halb zwölf.	Art begins at half past eleven.

Wochentage	**Days of the week**
Montag	Monday
Dienstag	Tuesday
Mittwoch	Wednesday
Donnerstag	Thursday
Freitag	Friday
Samstag	Saturday
Sonntag	Sunday

Checklist

How well do you think you can do the following? Write a sentence for each one if you can.	I can do this well	I can do this but not very well	I can't do this yet
1 say what's in your classroom and your schoolbag			
2 use der/die/das and einen/eine/ein correctly			
3 say which school subjects you have			
4 give your opinion on school subjects			
5 tell the time			
6 say the days of the week			

1 🎧 **Listen to these people saying what hobbies they have. Work out who is who and write the names.**

a

Sophie

c

e

g

i

b

d

f

h

j

Arzu	Dennis	Jessica	Marie	Sophie
Carsten	Heino	Lukas	Rebecca	Tim

2 **Read this paragraph. Choose five correct sentences from the list below and tick them.**

Hi! Ich heiße Marko. Ich spiele sehr gern Gitarre. Ich bin in einer Band. Ich spiele auch gern Schlagzeug, aber nicht so gut. Ich bin absolut nicht sportlich. Ich spiele nicht gern Tennis und ich spiele auch nicht gern Fußball. Meine Schwester Hilke ist sportlich, aber nicht musikalisch. Sie spielt gern Federball, aber nicht gern Geige.

a ✔ Marko likes playing guitar.

b ☐ He doesn't like playing the drums.

c ☐ He isn't sporty.

d ☐ He plays in a band.

e ☐ Hilke is sporty.

f ☐ She likes to play the violin.

g ☐ She likes playing badminton.

h ☐ She's in a band.

3 **Draw lines to link the words.**

ich   spielt

du   spielen

er   spielst

wir   spielt

ihr   spiele

sie   spielen

1 Insert numbers to show the correct word order in these jumbled sentences.
Remember: first the subject, then the verb.

a gehe Ich einkaufen gern

    2   1   4   3

_____

d Rad gern fahre Ich

_____

b Ich Internet gern chatte im

_____

e sehe Ich fern gern

_____

c höre Ich Musik gern

_____

f gern lese Ich

_____

2 Put ticks by each picture to show what Ali likes (✓),
prefers (✓✓) and likes best (✓✓✓).

a   ✓✓✓   **d**   [ ]

b   [ ]   **e**   [ ]

c   [ ]   **f**    [ ]

> gern ✓, lieber ✓✓, am liebsten ✓✓✓

3 Choose the correct verb form.

a Ich <u>fährst</u> / (<u>fahre</u>) nicht gern Skateboard.

b Er <u>spielt</u> / <u>spiele</u> gern Klavier.

c Claudia <u>höre</u> / <u>hört</u> am liebsten Rap.

d Ich <u>liest</u> / <u>lese</u> gern Bücher.

e Alfons <u>geht</u> / <u>gehen</u> lieber ins Kino.

f Du <u>spiele</u> / <u>spielst</u> nicht gern am Computer.

1 Complete this advert for a *ZOOM* computer game. Write in the correct words.

Lernst du Deutsch?

Das **ZOOM-Spiel** ist _____cool_____ (*cool*)!

Es ist _____ (*funny*) und _____ (*exciting*).

Das **ZOOM-Spiel** ist nicht _____ (*boring*).

Findest du Deutsch _____ (*terrible*)?

Nicht mit **ZOOM**.

Es ist _____ (*super*) und auch _____ (*useful*).

| schrecklich   cool   spannend   super   lustig   nützlich   langweilig |

2 🎧 What do these people think of each type of game?
Write the answer in English.

a

It is _____ .

c

It is _____ .

e

It is _____ .

b

It is _____ .

d

It is _____ .

f

It is _____ .

3 Unjumble the second half of each sentence.

a Ich mag Sportspiele, <u>sie super denn sind</u>.   Ich mag Sportspiele, ___denn sie sind super.___

b Ich mag Lernspiele nicht, <u>langweilig sie denn sind</u>.

   Ich mag Lernspiele nicht, _____

c Ich mag Musikspiele, <u>denn lustig sind sie</u>.   Ich mag Musikspiele, _____

d Ich mag Abenteuerspiele nicht, <u>sie denn schrecklich sind</u>.

   Ich mag Abenteuerspiele nicht, _____

1 Find the correct expression for each picture and write the correct letter in each box.

1	2	3	4	5
b				

a am Abend   c am Wochenende   e am Nachmittag
b am Montag   d jeden Tag

2 🎧 Listen and draw lines to link the activity with when it is done.

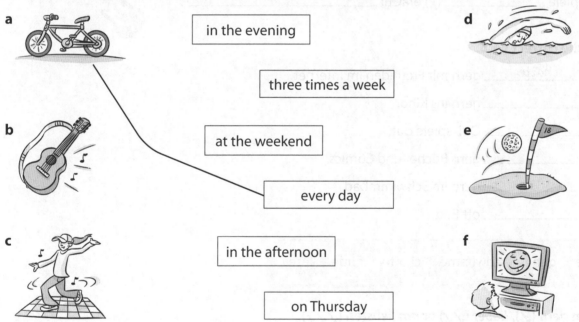

a

in the evening

three times a week

at the weekend

every day

in the afternoon

on Thursday

d

e

b

c

f

3 Fill in the gaps to show how often you do these things.
It doesn't have to be true!

a Ich spiele _____ am Computer.

b Ich sehe _____ fern.

c Ich fahre _____ Skateboard.

d Ich schwimme _____ .

jeden Tag	am Wochenende
am Abend	jeden Tag
am Nachmittag	zweimal in der Woche
am Montag	

2A.5 Am Wochenende

1 **Unscramble the hobby and write in _gern_ or _nicht gern_.**

a   Ich spiele _____gern_____ (✓) lgchSeaguz _____ .

b   Ich spiele _____ (✗) lbuFlßa _____ .

c   Ich spiele _____ (✓) lblyaVloel _____ .

d   Ich spiele _____ (✓) dblFlreea _____ .

e   Ich spiele _____ (✗) eraGtir _____ .

2 **Put in the correct verb.**

a   Ich _____chatte_____ gern mit Freunden im Internet.

b   Ich _____ gern ins Kino.

c   Ich _____ Quizspiele gut.

d   Ich _____ gern Bücher und Comics.

e   Ich _____ gern im Schwimmbad.

f   Ich _____ oft Rad.

> fahre   gehe   schwimme   chatte   finde   lese

3 **Write in _gern_ (✓), _lieber_ (✓✓) or _am liebsten_ (✓✓✓).**

a   Ich spiele _____lieber_____ (✓✓) am Computer.

b   Ich fahre _____ (✓✓✓) Skateboard.

c   Ich gehe _____ (✓) einkaufen.

d   Ich spiele _____ (✓✓) Abenteuerspiele.

e   Ich sehe _____ (✓✓✓) fern.

ich spiele – du spielst – er/sie/es spielt – wir spielen – ihr spielt – sie/Sie spielen

1 Interpret the pictures and decide on the person (*ich*, *du* etc.) and the verb form (*spiele* etc.).

a _____Ich_____ spiel_e_ Fußball.

b _____ spiel____ Tennis.

c Spiel____ _____ Gitarre?

d Spiel____ _____ am Computer?

e _____ spiel____ Schach.

f _____ spiel____ Klavier.

2 Draw lines to link the 'person' and the correct verb form.

ich	fahren	ich	liest
du	fahrt	du	lest
er / sie / es	fahre	er / sie / es	lesen
wir	fährt	wir	lese
ihr	fährst	ihr	lesen
sie / Sie	fahren	sie / Sie	liest

Positive or negative?

1 Write P (positive) or N (negative) by these words and expressions.

langweilig ☐ N   schlecht ☐

gut ☐   furchtbar ☐

super ☐   lustig ☐

gern ☐   prima ☐

nicht gern ☐   nicht so gut ☐

> Words are often used to show what attitudes we have. Working out whether somebody's opinion of something is positive or negative can often help you a lot when you are trying to understand what somebody is saying to you, or in a listening exercise.

Syllables

2 Put together the syllables to make the German words for sports and musical instruments. Insert them in the grid and identify the shaded word. Each word has been started for you.

```
a  R  U  G
      b  T  E  N
c  K  L  A  V
         d  G  I  T
e  S  C  H  W  I  M  M
```

| E N | | B Y | | E |
| IER | | NIS | | ARR |

The shaded word is _____ . It means _____ .

> German is a language where all the syllables in a word are pronounced. This makes reading simple because you just pronounce what you see on the page.

'e' at the end of a word

3 Say these words out loud.

Schlange, fahre, spiele, sehe, Hunde, Freunde, gehe, Gitarre

P.S. In that list, can you spot …

- two singular nouns? _____

- two plural nouns? _____

> In English, an 'e' at the end of a word isn't normally pronounced (game, bottle, cassette). In German, you do pronounce it. It sounds a bit like 'uh'.

2A Vokabular

Ich spiele (nicht) gern …	I (don't) like playing …
Spielst du gern …?	Do you like playing …?
Basketball	basketball
Federball	badminton
Fußball	football
Rugby	rugby
Tennis	tennis
Volleyball	volleyball
Flöte	flute
Geige	violin
Gitarre	guitar
Klavier	piano
Schlagzeug	drums
am Computer	on the computer
in einer Band	in a band
Karten	cards
Schach	chess

Das mache ich am liebsten	That's what I like doing most of all
Ich besuche gern meine Freunde.	I like visiting my friends.
Ich chatte gern im Internet.	I like chatting on the internet.
Ich sehe gern fern.	I like watching TV.
Ich gehe gern ins Kino.	I like going to the cinema.
Ich gehe gern ins Café.	I like going to the café.
Ich gehe gern einkaufen.	I like going shopping.
Ich fahre gern Rad.	I like cycling.
Ich fahre gern Skateboard.	I like skateboarding.
Ich fahre gern Ski.	I like skiing.
Ich höre gern Musik.	I like listening to music.
Ich lese gern.	I like reading.
Ich tanze gern.	I like dancing.
Ich schwimme gern.	I like swimming.
Ich sehe lieber fern.	I prefer watching TV.
Ich spiele am liebsten Rugby.	Most of all I like playing rugby.
Ich sehe mir gern (Rugby) im Fernsehen an.	I like watching (rugby) on TV.

Ich liebe Computerspiele	I love computer games
das Abenteuerspiel	adventure game
das Lernspiel	educational game
das Musikspiel	music game
das Quizspiel	quiz game
das Sportspiel	sports game
das Tanzspiel	dance game
Magst du (Sportspiele)?	Do you like (sports games)?
Wie findest du (Quizspiele)?	How do you find (quiz games)?
Ich mag … (nicht).	I (don't) like …
…, denn ich finde sie …	…, because I find them …
anstrengend	tiring, strenuous
cool	cool
klasse	great

interessant	interesting
langweilig	boring
lustig	funny
nützlich	useful
schrecklich	awful, terrible
schwierig	difficult
spannend	exciting
toll	great

Wie oft machst du das?	How often do you do that?
am Montag, Dienstag, …	on Monday, Tuesday, …
am Wochenende	at the weekend
am Morgen	in the morning
am Nachmittag	in the afternoon
am Abend	in the evening
jeden Tag	every day
jeden Monat	every month
jede Woche	every week
jedes Jahr	every year
einmal/zweimal/dreimal in der Woche	once/twice/three times a week
Ich höre jeden Tag Musik.	I listen to music every day.

Checklist

How well do you think you can do the following?			
Write a sentence for each one if you can.			
	I can do this well	I can do this but not very well	I can't do this yet
1 say what your hobbies are (sport, music)			
2 use gern, lieber, am liebsten			
3 use irregular verbs like lesen, sehen and fahren			
4 give your opinions on hobbies			
5 use denn to mean because			
6 use expressions of time and frequency			

1 🎧 **Listen and write the names of the cities in the right places.**

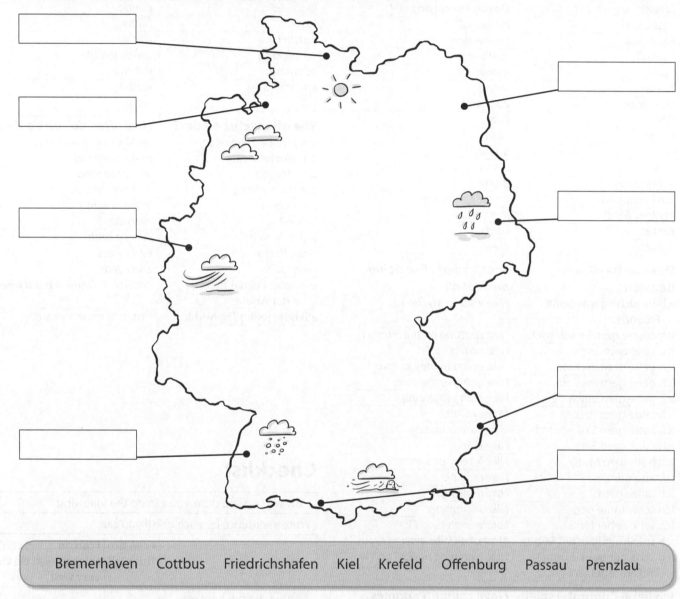

| Bremerhaven | Cottbus | Friedrichshafen | Kiel | Krefeld | Offenburg | Passau | Prenzlau |

2 **What's the weather like in these places? Circle the right phrase.**

Im Norden: (Es ist sonnig.) / Es regnet.

Im Nordwesten: Es ist sonnig. / Es ist wolkig.

Im Süden: Es ist kalt. / Es regnet.

Im Westen: Es regnet. / Es ist windig.

Im Osten: Es schneit. / Es regnet.

Im Südwesten: Es schneit. / Es ist neblig.

1 🎧 **Listen to these people saying where they live. Write a, b, c or d next to the correct picture.**

☐	☐	☐ *a*	☐
Dorf	**Stadt**	**Wohnsiedlung**	**Land**

2 **Decide whether these adjectives are positive or negative and write them in the correct columns.**

> furchtbar   toll   interessant   laut   super   langweilig   schön   nicht gut

Positive   **Negative**

_____toll_____   _____

_____   _____

_____   _____

_____   _____

3 🎧 **Now listen again and circle *richtig* (true) or *falsch* (false).**

a This boy likes where he lives.   richtig / (falsch)

b This girl likes where she lives.   richtig / falsch

c This boy likes where he lives.   richtig / falsch

d This girl likes where she lives.   richtig / falsch

4 **Complete these two sentences, one saying where you live and one saying what you think of it.**

Ich wohne _____.

Es ist _____.

1 🎧 **Listen and write in the numbers.**

a

_85_ Jahre alt

c

_____ Schüler

e

Nummer _____

g

Nummer _____

b

_____ €

d

_____ Bücher

f

_____ Bonbons

h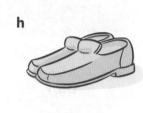

Größe _____

2 **Solve the clues and fill in the crossword.**

Waagerecht (across)

2 Where's my car?

4 Eat here

5 Oh Romeo!

7 Get wet here

8 Going underground

Senkrecht (down)

1 A room to get clean in.

3 For playing outside

6 What's cooking?

Badezimmer   Balkon

Dusche   Esszimmer   Garage

Garten   Keller   Küche

1 Unjumble the words and write them in.

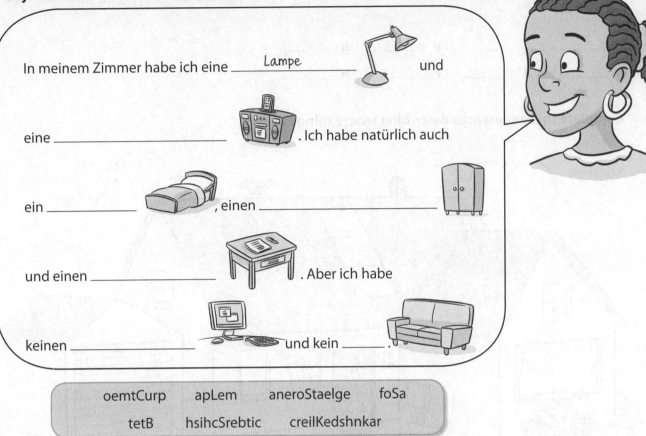

In meinem Zimmer habe ich eine _____ Lampe _____ und

eine _____ . Ich habe natürlich auch

ein _____ , einen _____

und einen _____ . Aber ich habe

keinen _____ und kein _____ .

oemtCurp	apLem	aneroStaelge	foSa
tetB	hsihcSrebtic	creilKedshnkar	

2 🎧 A different room is being described. Identify where the items are and circle the correct words.

a The lamp is ⟨on⟩ next to under the desk.

b The cat is on next to under the bed.

c The football is behind in front of next to the wardrobe.

d The bed is in front of next to behind the sofa.

e The computer is between the lamp and the stereo

behind the stereo in front of the lamp.

3 Complete the sentences to describe what's in your own room. Make sure you use words that fit – check whether it should be *ein*, *eine* or *einen*.

In meinem Zimmer gibt es einen _____ und

eine _____ .

Es gibt auch ein _____ und ein _____ .

1 🎧 **Listen to these numbers and write them down (just the figures, not the words).**

a ___55___ c _____ e _____ g _____

b _____ d _____ f _____ h _____

2 **Complete these sentences describing where things are.**

Der Vogel sitzt _____*auf*_____ dem Haus.

Nils ist _____ Haus.

Der Keller ist _____ dem Haus.

Die Garage ist _____ dem Haus.

Das Rad ist _____ dem Haus.

im   neben   hinter   vor   unter

1 Write in *der* or *dem*.

> After these prepositions: *in, auf, hinter, neben, vor, unter, zwischen*:
> masculine   dem
> feminine   der
> neuter   dem

a auf _____dem_____ Tisch

b unter _____ Stuhl

c neben _____ Schrank

d in _____ Tasche

e vor _____ Schule

f hinter _____ Tür

g zwischen _____ Haus und _____ Garage

h vor _____ Supermarkt

i _____ Auto

j vor _____ Post

der (m)	die (f)	das (n)
Tisch	Tasche	Haus
Stuhl	Tür	Auto
Schrank	Garage	
Supermarkt	Post	

2 Circle the correct word.

	masculine	feminine	neuter
Es gibt	einen	eine	ein

a In meiner Schule gibt es   einen / (eine) / ein   Bibliothek.

b In meiner Schule gibt es   einen / eine / ein   Schulhof.

c In meinem Haus gibt es   einen / eine / ein   Küche.

d In meinem Haus gibt es   einen / eine / ein   Wohnzimmer.

e In meinem Haus gibt es   einen / eine / ein   Badezimmer.

f In meiner Stadt gibt es   einen / eine / ein   Supermarkt.

g In meiner Stadt gibt es   einen / eine / ein   Kathedrale.

masculine	feminine	neuter
Schulhof	Bibliothek	Wohnzimmer
Supermarkt	Küche	Badezimmer
	Kathedrale	

1 🎧 Listen to the words. Put a tick if you hear the sound 'ch' and a cross if you don't.

a [X]   c [ ]   e [ ]   g [ ]   i [ ]
b [ ]   d [ ]   f [ ]   h [ ]   j [ ]

2 🎧 Listen again and jot down the words as you go. Then say them out loud. Finally, check that you have spelled them correctly.

a _____   f _____

b _____   g _____

c _____   h _____

d _____   i _____

e _____   j _____

3 Look back to the previous page (*Sprachlabor*). There are at least three nouns you haven't seen before but you can immediately work out what they mean. What are they?

_____

_____

> Because German is such a logical language, and similar in many ways to English, it's often easy to work out meanings.

4 Practise using the correct words for 'a' in this sentence.

> In meiner Tasche habe ich ___eine___ Zeitschrift,
> _____ Buch, _____ Teddy, _____ Handy,
> _____ DVD-Spieler, und _____ Maus!

masculine	feminine	neuter
DVD-Spieler	Zeitschrift	Handy
Teddy	Maus	Buch

> You can use correct articles even if you have never seen the words, as long as you know the gender. If the noun is masculine, use *einen*. If it's feminine, use *eine* and if it's neuter, use *ein*. Easy!

Remember also:
du – only use with family members, friends or adults with whom you have agreed to say *du* because you know them really well.
Sie – to any adult you don't know. It is very rude to say *du* to them.
ihr – when talking to two or more people you would normally call *du*.

> P.S. It is very important to know genders in German. Make sure you always note the gender of any new noun you learn.

Meine Region	**My region**
im Norden	in the north
im Nordosten	in the north-east
im Nordwesten	in the north-west
im Osten	in the east
im Süden	in the south
im Südosten	in the south-east
im Südwesten	in the south-west
im Westen	in the west

Das Wetter	**The weather**
Es ist heiß/kalt.	It is hot/cold.
neblig, windig, wolkig	foggy, windy, cloudy
schön, sonnig, warm	nice, sunny, warm
Es friert.	It's freezing/It freezes.
Es gewittert.	There's thunder and lightning.
Es regnet.	It's raining/It rains.
Es schneit.	It's snowing/It snows.
Es (regnet) nicht.	It isn't (raining)/It doesn't (rain).

Wo wohnst du?	**Where do you live?**
ich wohne	I live
du wohnst	you live
er/sie wohnt	he/she lives
wir wohnen	we live
ihr wohnt	you live (plural)
sie wohnen	they live
Sie wohnen	you live (formal)
am Stadtrand	on the edge of town
auf dem Land	in the countryside
in der Stadt	in town
in einem Bungalow	in a bungalow
in einem Doppelhaus	in a semi-detached house
in einem Dorf	in a village
in einem Einfamilienhaus	in a detached house
in einem Haus	in a house
in einem Reihenhaus	in a terraced house
in einer Wohnsiedlung	on a housing estate
in einer Wohnung	in a flat

Wie ist es?	**What is it like?**
grün	green
interessant, langweilig	interesting, boring
laut	noisy, loud
praktisch	practical
schön, toll	beautiful, great

Mein Haus	**My house**
der Balkon	balcony
der Garten	garden
der Keller	cellar
die Dusche	shower
die Garage	garage
die Küche	kitchen

das Badezimmer	bathroom
das Esszimmer	dining room
das Schlafzimmer	bedroom
das Wohnzimmer	living room
im Erdgeschoss	on the ground floor
im ersten/zweiten Stock	on the first/second floor

Mein Zimmer	**My room**
In meinem Zimmer gibt es …	In my room there is …
einen Computer	a computer
einen Fernseher	a TV
einen Kleiderschrank	a wardrobe
einen Schreibtisch	a desk
einen Stuhl	a chair
eine Lampe	a lamp
eine Stereoanlage	a hi-fi system
ein Bett	a bed
ein Poster	a poster
ein Regal	a shelf
ein Sofa	a sofa
auf	on
hinter	behind
im	in the
neben	next to
unter	under
vor	in front of
zwischen	between

Zahlen	**Numbers**
zweiunddreißig	thirty-two
vierzig, fünfzig, sechzig	forty, fifty, sixty
siebzig, achtzig, neunzig	seventy, eighty, ninety
hundert	hundred

Checklist

How well do you think you can do the following?			
Write a sentence for each one if you can.			
	I can do this well	I can do this but not very well	I can't do this yet
1 say where you live			
2 say what the weather is like			
3 describe your house or flat			
4 say what's in your room			
5 count up to a hundred			
6 use *auf*, *in*, *hinter*, *neben*, *vor*, *zwischen* and *unter* correctly			

3A.1 Was isst du gern?

1 Draw lines to link the words to the items in the fridge.

Salat

Hähnchen

Cola

Orangensaft

Fisch

Käse

Joghurt

Milch

Wasser

2 Put a tick or a cross to show what these people like and dislike.

a Nils:

b Susanne:

3 Circle the correct word order. Remember, the verb always comes second.

a Zum Frühstück   ich esse / esse ich   Cornflakes.

b Zum Mittagessen   esse ich / ich esse   eine Banane.

c Zum Abendessen   ich trinke / trinke ich   Wasser.

1 Draw lines to show where you would buy these items.

  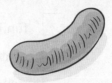 

 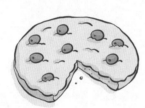  

2 🎧 Listen and work out where these people are.
Write *PIZZERIA, EISDIELE, IMBISS* or *BÄCKEREI*.

a   IMBISS _____

b   _____

c   _____

d   _____

e   _____

f   _____

g   _____

h   _____

3 🎧 Listen again and write down, in English, what the people are ordering.

a   curried sausage with chips _____

b   _____

c   _____

d   _____

e   _____

f   _____

g   _____

h   _____

1 🎧 **Listen to some large numbers. In the boxes next to the numbers here, write the order you hear them in. The first one is done for you.**

☐	dreihundertzwanzig	☐	fünfhundertsechsundsechzig
☐	zweihundertdreißig	☐	achthundertvierundzwanzig
a	tausend	☐	siebenhunderteinundvierzig
☐	hundertachtzig	☐	neunhundert
☐	vierhundertfünfzig	☐	sechshunderteinundneunzig

2 **Circle the appropriate words.**

a Ich möchte ⟨einen Becher⟩ / ein Pfund   Joghurt.

b Ich möchte   eine Packung / ein Glas   Cornflakes.

c Ich möchte   500 Gramm / eine Flasche   Cola.

d Ich möchte   eine Dose / eine Tüte   Brötchen.

e Ich möchte   einen Liter / eine Scheibe   Milch.

f Ich möchte   ein Kilo / eine Flasche   Orangensaft.

3 **Make a shopping list with these items.**

Einkaufsliste

Ich möchte ...

eine Dose Cola

_____

_____

_____

_____

_____

500g

Wasser	sechs	eine Dose	einen Liter
Schinken	Cola	500 Gramm	Bananen
eine Flasche	Joghurt	Milch	einen Becher

3A.4 Ich esse kein Fleisch

1 Herr Gierig and Frau Gierig have completely opposite tastes.
Complete the sentences using *keinen*, *keine* or *kein*.

Herr Gierig: Ich esse gern Bonbons.

Frau Gierig: Und ich esse _____keine_____ Bonbons.

Herr Gierig: Ich esse gern Schokolade.

Frau Gierig: Und ich esse _____ Schokolade.

Herr Gierig: Ich esse gern Pommes.

Frau Gierig: Ich esse _____ Pommes.

Herr Gierig: Ich esse gern Fleisch.

Frau Gierig: Ich esse _____ Fleisch.

Herr Gierig: Ich esse gern Apfelkuchen.

Frau Gierig: Ich esse _____ Apfelkuchen.

Herr Gierig: Ich trinke gern Cola.

Frau Gierig: Ich trinke _____ Cola.

masculine	Apfelkuchen
feminine	Schokolade, Cola
neuter	Fleisch
plural	Pommes, Bonbons

2 🎧 Listen to these people and write, in English, what they don't eat and why.

	What?	**Why?**
a	fish	_____
b	_____	_____
c	_____	_____
d	_____	_____
e	_____	_____

3 Look at Activity 1 again. Give Herr Gierig some good health advice,
using *Man soll* … Go through all the things he eats and drinks.

a _____Man soll keine Bonbons essen._____

b _____

c _____

d _____

e _____

f _____

3A.5 Nicos Videoblog

1 **Draw lines to the items. Each item needs two lines, one for its name and one for the amount.**

eine Dose

sechs Scheiben

eine Flasche

ein Becher

eine Packung

ein Glas

2 Kilo

Erdbeermarmelade

Kartoffeln

Suppe

Chips

Mineralwasser

Joghurt

Schinken

2 **Write sentences to show these people's opinions of food.**

a Ich esse gern Bratwurst.

b _____

c _____

d _____

e _____

f _____

> Ich esse gern / nicht gern …
> Ich esse keinen / keine / kein …

3 🎧 **Listen to the interview and fill in the gaps in the text in English.**

Lukas likes ____muesli____ for breakfast because _____ .

He doesn't like _____ , because _____ .

He drinks _____ or _____ but not _____ .

He eats _____ and _____ at lunch time but his sister

doesn't approve. She says _____ .

In the evening, Lukas eats _____ or _____

but not _____ or _____ .

1 Unjumble these sentences and write the words out in the correct order. Always start with the meal. Remember, the verb is always the second piece of information.

a Cornflakes Zum esse Frühstück ich   _Zum Frühstück esse ich Cornflakes._

b Abendessen Brot esse Zum ich _____

c Kaffee ich Zum trinke Frühstück _____

d Mittagessen ich Zum esse Salat _____

e Wasser Zum trinke Abendessen ich _____

f trinke Mittagessen Zum Orangensaft ich.

_____

2 Tell these people off for their bad habits. Use *man soll* and *keinen*, *keine* or *kein*.

a Ich esse gern Bratwurst.   _Man soll keine Bratwurst essen._

b Ich spiele gern Computerspiele. _____

c Ich trinke gern Whisky. _____

d Ich fahre gern Motorrad. _____

e Ich esse gern Schokolade. _____

f Ich trinke gern Bier. _____

masculine	feminine	neuter	plural
Whisky	Bratwurst	Motorrad	Computerspiele
	Schokolade	Bier	

3 Choose whether the linking words in these sentences mean 'and', 'or', 'but' or 'because'.

a Ich esse keinen Fisch, denn ich finde Fisch furchtbar. (and / or / but / (because))

b Ich spiele Hockey und ich spiele auch Tennis.   (and / or / but / because)

c Ich esse gern Salat, aber ich esse nicht gern Fleisch.   (and / or / but / because)

d Spielen wir am Computer oder gehen wir essen?   (and / or / but / because)

e Opa fährt nach Frankreich oder nach Schweden.   (and / or / but / because)

f Sonja mag gern Physik und Chemie.   (and / or / but / because)

g Olaf mag gern Chemie, aber nicht Physik.   (and / or / but / because)

h Wir lernen gern Deutsch, denn es macht Spaß.   (and / or / but / because)

3A.6B Think

Linking words

1 **What words should link these sentences?**

  a Möchtest du Reis _____ Nudeln? (*or*)

  b Wir mögen Musik _____ Kunst. (*and*)

  c Ich möchte Bratwurst _____ keine Pommes. (*but*)

  d Ich spiele gut Fußball _____ nicht so gut Tennis. (*but*)

  e Ich schwimme gern, _____ ich bin sportlich. (*because*)

  f Wir mögen Cola, _____ es ist besser als Wasser. (*because*)

  g Ich trinke Kaffee _____ Tee. (*and*)

  h Möchtest du Käse _____ Wurst? (*or*)

> To make your language sound more natural and less simple, try to use words to link sentences together. In this unit, four linking words are used. Can you remember them?

Pronunciation

2 **Say these words out loud and put them into the correct column.**

> Nudeln Hund Schule du Mutter Joghurt zum
> Butter Erdkunde Musik Kunst Bruder Stuhl Bus

short 'u'

Hund _____ _____

_____ _____

_____

long 'u'

Nudeln _____ _____

_____ _____

_____

> The vowel 'u' is pronounced in two different ways, as a 'short' vowel or a 'long' vowel.

Politeness

3 **Put these words into the correct column.**

> Ein Eis! Ich möchte ein Eis, bitte! Nein. Ja. Ja, bitte. Nein, danke.
> Ein Eis, bitte. Bitte schön. Danke schön. Ja? Hier!

polite

Ich möchte ein Eis, bitte! _____

_____

_____

_____

not so polite

Ein Eis! _____

_____

_____

_____

> In German, it is very important to be polite. This means saying *ich möchte* … rather than just saying the word, and using *bitte* and *danke* (just like in English!).

Essen und Trinken — *Food and drink*

Essen und Trinken	Food and drink
Was isst du gern/nicht gern?	*What do/don't you like eating?*
Ich esse gern/nicht gern …	*I like/don't like eating …*
Brot	*bread*
ein Ei	*an egg*
eine Banane, einen Apfel	*a banana, an apple*
Fisch	*fish*
Hähnchen	*chicken*
Joghurt	*yoghurt*
Kartoffeln	*potatoes*
Käse	*cheese*
Nudeln	*pasta*
Reis	*rice*
Salat	*salad*
Was trinkst du gern/nicht gern?	*What do/don't you like drinking?*
Ich trinke gern/nicht gern …	*I like/don't like drinking …*
Cola	*cola*
Milch	*milk*
Orangensaft	*orange juice*

Mahlzeiten — *Meals*

Mahlzeiten	Meals
Was isst/trinkst du …	*What do you eat/drink …*
zum Frühstück?	*for breakfast?*
zum Mittagessen?	*for lunch?*
zum Abendessen?	*for dinner?*
Zum Frühstück esse ich …	*For breakfast I eat …*
Zum Mittagessen trinke ich …	*For lunch I drink …*
Zum Abendessen …	*For dinner …*
Butter	*butter*
Cornflakes	*cornflakes*
Müsli	*muesli*
Marmelade	*jam*
Kaffee, Tee, Wasser	*coffee, tea, water*
meistens	*mostly*
normalerweise	*usually*

Etwas zu essen — *Ordering food*

Etwas zu essen	Ordering food
Was darf es sein?	*What would you like?*
Was möchtest du?	*What would you like?*
Ja bitte?	*Yes, please?*
Kann ich Ihnen helfen?	*Can I help you?*
Ich möchte/nehme …, bitte.	*I'd like …, please.*
ein Erdbeereis	*a strawberry ice cream*
ein Schokoladeneis	*a chocolate ice cream*
ein Vanilleeis	*a vanilla ice cream*
mit/ohne Sahne	*with/without cream*
Pizza mit …	*pizza with …*
Oliven/Pilzen/Spinat	*olives/mushrooms/spinach*
Thunfisch/Tomaten/Zwiebeln	*tuna/tomatoes/onions*
Apfelkuchen	*apple cake*
Bio-Brot	*organic bread*
Bratwurst	*fried sausage*

Brötchen	*bread rolls*
Currywurst	*curried sausage*
Hamburger	*hamburger*
mit Mayonnaise/Ketchup	*with mayonnaise/ketchup*
Pommes frites	*fries*
Schwarzwälder Kirschtorte	*Black Forest gateau*

Im Geschäft — *In the shop*

Im Geschäft	In the shop
Sonst noch etwas?	*Anything else?*
Nein danke, das ist alles.	*No thanks, that's all.*
250 Gramm	*250 grams*
ein (halbes) Pfund	*(half) a pound*
ein (halbes) Kilo	*(half) a kilo*
ein Glas Marmelade	*a jar of jam*
ein Stück Käse	*a piece of cheese*
eine Dose Cola	*a can of cola*
eine Flasche Wasser	*a bottle of water*
eine Packung Kaffee	*a packet of coffee*
eine Scheibe Schinken	*a slice of ham*
eine Tüte Brötchen	*a bag of bread rolls*
einen Becher Joghurt	*a pot of yoghurt*
einen Liter Milch	*a litre of milk*

Ich esse kein Fleisch — *I don't eat meat*

Ich esse kein Fleisch	I don't eat meat
Man soll … essen/trinken.	*You should eat/drink …*
Man soll keinen/keine/kein … essen/trinken.	*You shouldn't eat/drink …*
Chips	*crisps*
Fastfood	*fast food*
Fleisch	*meat*
Gemüse	*vegetables*
Kuchen	*cake*
Obst	*fruit*
Schokolade	*chocolate*

Checklist

How well do you think you can do the following?			
Write a sentence for each one if you can.			
	I can do this well	I can do this but not very well	I can't do this yet
1 say what you like and don't like to eat and drink			
2 order food at a food stall			
3 buy food in a shop			
4 say how much you'd like			
5 count up to 1000			
6 use *sollen* correctly			

1 Solve the clues and fill in the crossword.

Waagerecht (across)
- **1** A place to do the weekly shopping
- **4** A place to buy stamps
- **6** Wet and wild
- **8** Good for a football match
- **9** A place to worship
- **10** Full of animals

Senkrecht (down)
- **1** A big, ancient building
- **2** A place for grass and trees
- **3** You can see a film here
- **5** A place to catch a train
- **7** Full of old things

Bahnhof   Kino
Kirche   Museum
Post   Park   Schloss
Schwimmbad   Stadion
Supermarkt   Zoo

Stadtpuzzle

2 Put numbers in the boxes to show the order in which you hear the places mentioned. Anything not mentioned, leave blank.

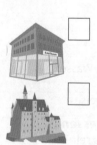

3 Listen again. Note, in English, which places don't exist in this town.

_____   _____

4 Choose the correct word for 'a'.

a Es gibt (einen) / eine / ein Park.

b Es gibt einen / eine / ein Kaufhaus.

c Es gibt einen / eine / ein Kirche.

d Es gibt einen / eine / ein Supermarkt.

e Es gibt einen / eine / ein Kino.

f Es gibt einen / eine / ein Bahnhof.

masculine	feminine	neuter
Park	Kirche	Kaufhaus
Supermarkt		Kino
Bahnhof		

1 **Where can you do these things? Write in the right number.**

 PIZZERIA **1**
 STADION **2**
 JUGEND-ZENTRUM **3**
 CAFÉ **4**
 SCHWIMMBAD **5**
 SKATEBOARD-BAHN **6**
 DISCO **7**
 KINO **8**

a [3] Man kann hier Freunde treffen.

b [ ] Man kann hier Kaffee trinken.

c [ ] Man kann hier tanzen.

d [ ] Man kann hier Pizza essen.

e [ ] Man kann hier Fußball spielen.

f [ ] Man kann hier einen Film sehen.

g [ ] Man kann hier schwimmen.

h [ ] Man kann hier Skateboard fahren.

2 **Listen to Claudia describing Schwerin. Circle *falsch* (false) or *richtig* (true).**

a Schwerin is boring. (falsch) / richtig

b There's a park and a castle. falsch / richtig

c You can play football in the park. falsch / richtig

d You can cycle in the park. falsch / richtig

e Table tennis is not allowed. falsch / richtig

f There are restaurants but no cinema. falsch / richtig

g Schwerin is a good place to eat out. falsch / richtig

h It's in South Germany. falsch / richtig

3 **Complete the sentences:**

a Es gibt __ein Restaurant__ . Man kann hier _____ .

b Es gibt _____ . Man kann hier _____ .

c Es gibt _____ . Man kann hier _____ .

d Es gibt _____ . Man kann hier _____ .

e Es gibt _____ . Man kann hier _____ .

| Löwen sehen | Englisch lernen | ein Restaurant | ein Kino | Fußball spielen |
| einen Park | essen | eine Schule | einen Film sehen | einen Zoo |

3B.3 Wo ist das Kino?

1 **Draw lines to link the directions to the pictures.**

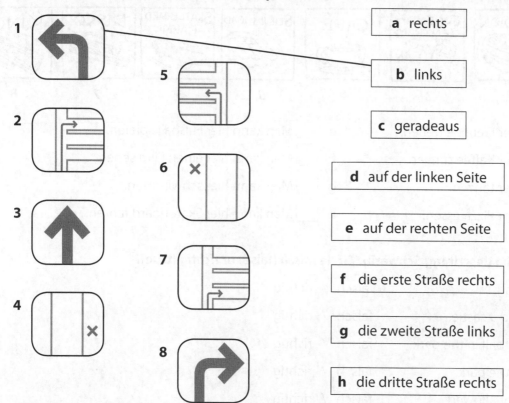

a rechts

b links

c geradeaus

d auf der linken Seite

e auf der rechten Seite

f die erste Straße rechts

g die zweite Straße links

h die dritte Straße rechts

2 🎧 **Use the pictures in Activity 1 again. Listen and write in the numbers for the instructions given.**

a __5__   c _____   e _____   g _____

b _____   d _____   f _____   h _____

3 **Write in the names of the places.**

a Der Bahnhof? Nehmen Sie die erste Straße links.

b Das Kaufhaus? Nehmen Sie die zweite Straße rechts.

c Das Schwimmbad? Gehen Sie geradeaus.

d Die Post? Nehmen Sie die erste Straße rechts.

e Das Schloss? Nehmen Sie die zweite Straße links.

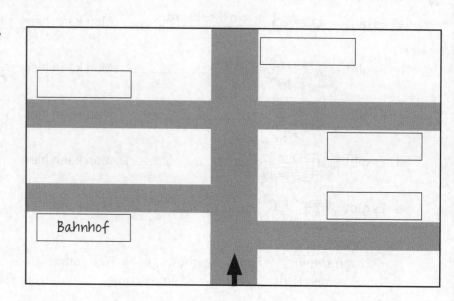

1 Draw lines to link the words to the pictures.

a

drei Karten

b

zwei Kinder

c

zwei Erwachsene und ein Kind

d

vier Kinder

e

zwei Karten

f

drei Erwachsene

2 What do these people want? Write the answers in English.

a _a book_

b _____

c _____

d _____

e _____

f _____

3 Unjumble these questions so the words are in the right order.

a Buch ein du Möchtest?   _Möchtest du ein Buch?_

b Handy du ein Möchtest?   _____

c eine Möchtest Bratwurst du?   _____

d Erdbeereis du ein Möchtest?   _____

e einen Möchtest Schlüsselanhänger du?   _____

f ein du Möchtest Geschenk?   _____

1 **Put a tick or a cross by these sentences to show whether they are true or not.**

Was gibt es in Dösdorf?

a ☒ Es gibt ein Kaufhaus.

b ☐ Es gibt keinen Supermarkt.

c ☐ Es gibt keine Kirche.

d ☐ Es gibt ein Schloss.

e ☐ Es gibt eine Skateboard-Bahn.

f ☐ Es gibt einen Bahnhof.

g ☐ Es gibt einen Fernsehturm.

2 🎧 **Listen to Ergül talking about Delmenhorst, the town where he lives. Answer the questions with 'Yes' or 'No'.**

a Is Delmenhorst big? __No__

b Can you swim there? _____

c Does Ergül like skateboarding? _____

d Can he go to the cinema in Delmenhorst? _____

e Is there a football stadium in Delmenhorst? _____

f Is there one in Bremen? _____

3 **Write the instructions next to each picture.**

a _Nehmen Sie die dritte Straße links._

b _____

c _____

d _____

e _____

f _____

> Nehmen Sie …
> die erste / zweite / dritte Straße
> links / rechts.
> Gehen Sie geradeaus.
> Gehen Sie links / rechts.

1 Circle the correct word.

a Ich   können / könnt / (kann) schwimmen.

b Er   willst / wollen / will   Eis essen.

c Wir   können / kann / kannst   Deutsch sprechen.

d Roberta   kannst / kann / könnt   Gitarre spielen.

e Will / Willst / Wollt   du ins Kino gehen?

f Mutti und Vati   will / wollen / wollt   nach Kiel fahren.

	können	wollen
ich	kann	will
du	kannst	willst
er/sie/es	kann	will
wir	können	wollen
ihr	könnt	wollt
sie/Sie	können	wollen

2 Choose words from below to fill the gaps in these instructions.

a ___Gehen Sie___ geradeaus. (*go*)

b _____ keine Pommes. (*eat*)

c _____ die erste Straße links. (*take*)

d _____ mit dem Rad. (*go*)

e _____ nach Berlin. (*come*)

f _____ ein Geschenk. (*buy*)

> Fahren Sie   Nimm   Gehen Sie   Kommen Sie   Kauf   Iss

3 Now write down the letters of the instructions in Activity 2 which are:

a given to an adult. _____

b given to a child or friend. _____

4 🎧 Say these words out loud. Some you know, some you will have to work out. Then listen to the recording to check you got them right.

> Achterbahn   will   wild   voll   sprechen
> schwimmen   wohne   wollen   besuchen
> möchte   Schloss   Weimar   vielleicht   bevor

Sentence patterns

1 Read the advert and write, beside each sentence, INVITATION, YOU CAN or THERE IS.

a Kommen Sie nach <u>Soltau</u>!   <u>INVITATION</u>

b Besuchen Sie <u>den Heide-Park</u>!   _____

c Fahren Sie <u>Karussell</u>!   _____

d Essen Sie <u>Zuckerwatte</u>*!   _____

e Kaufen Sie <u>Souvenirs</u>!   _____

f Es gibt <u>viele Attraktionen</u>.   _____

g Es gibt viel für Kinder.   _____

h Man kann <u>Achterbahn</u>* fahren.   _____

i Man kann <u>Krokodile</u> sehen.   _____

> * Zuckerwatte
> – candy floss
> * Achterbahn
> – roller coaster

> Looking at the structure of sentences can give you clues as to what they are saying. In this unit we had:
> - sentences which are invitations (*Kommen Sie …! Besuchen Sie …!*)
> - sentences saying what you can do (*Man kann …*)
> - sentences saying what there is (*Es gibt …*).

Adapting texts

2 Read the advert again. Write an advert for a different place. Use the sentences in the advert and change the details to those below.

_____

_____

_____

_____

_____

_____

_____

_____

> It is easy to create your own texts by adapting existing ones and changing some of the content.

> * Bimmelbahn
> – little train
> * Aal – eel
> * Pferdekutsche
> – horse and carriage

> Worpswede   die Galerien   Bimmelbahn*   Aal*
> Postkarten   alte Häuser   Pferdekutsche*   Künstler

3 What kind of place is …

a the Heide-Park Soltau?   _____

b Worpswede?   _____

4 What do you think a *Künstler* is?
Your knowledge of school subjects will help.

Was gibt es? / *What is there?*

Es gibt (keinen/keine/kein) …	There is (no) …/There are (no) …
Gibt es …?	Is there …?
einen Bahnhof	a railway station
einen Fernsehturm	a TV tower
ein Geschäft	a shop
ein Jugendzentrum	a youth centre
ein Kaufhaus	a department store
ein Kino	a cinema
eine Kirche	a church
ein Museum	a museum
einen Park	a park
ein Schloss	a castle
ein Schwimmbad	a swimming pool
ein Stadion	a stadium
einen Supermarkt	a supermarket
eine Post	a post office
eine Skateboard-Bahn	a skatepark
eine U-Bahn-Station	an underground station
einen Zoo	a zoo

Was kann man machen? / *What can one do?*

Man kann (nicht) …	One can (not) …
Ich kann …	I can …
Kannst du …?	Can you …?
Freunde treffen	meet friends
Fußball spielen	play football
in der Disco tanzen	dance in the disco
ins Kino gehen	go to the cinema
ins Theater gehen	go to the theatre
Kaffee trinken	drink coffee
Pizza essen	eat pizza
Rad fahren	cycle
schwimmen	swim

Wo ist …? / *Where is …?*

der Bahnhof	the railway station
der Park	the park
die Post	the post office
das Schloss	the castle
das Schwimmbad	the swimming pool
die Skateboard-Bahn	the skatepark
das Stadion	the stadium
der Supermarkt	the supermarket

Richtungen / *Directions*

Geh …	Go … (informal)
Gehen Sie …	Go … (formal)
Nimm …	Take … (informal)
Nehmen Sie …	Take … (formal)
links	left
rechts	right
geradeaus	straight on

die erste Straße	the first road
die zweite Straße	the second road
die dritte Straße	the third road
über die Ampel	over the traffic lights
über die Kreuzung	over the crossing
über die Brücke	over the bridge
auf der linken Seite	on the left-hand side
auf der rechten Seite	on the right-hand side

Im Zoo / *At the zoo*

Ich möchte …	I'd like …
eine Karte	a ticket
zwei Karten	two tickets
für ein Kind	for a child
für zwei Kinder	for two children
für einen Erwachsenen	for an adult
für zwei Erwachsene	for two adults
Was kostet das?	How much does it cost?
Das kostet …	That costs …
Danke (schön).	Thank you.
Bitte (schön).	You're welcome.

Im Souvenirladen / *In the souvenir shop*

der Lolli	lollipop
das Notizbuch	notebook
die Plastikschlange	plastic snake
der Schlüsselanhänger	key ring
die Schneekugel	snow globe
die Schachtel Schokolade	box of chocolates
Ich suche …	I am looking for …
ein Geschenk	a present
Ich kaufe einen/eine/ein …	I (will) buy a …
Ich nehme einen/eine/ein …	I (will) take a …
Ich möchte einen/eine/ein …	I would like a …

Checklist

How well do you think you can do the following? Write a sentence for each one if you can.	I can do this well	I can do this but not very well	I can't do this yet
1 say what there is in a town			
2 say what you can do in a town			
3 give opinions about places			
4 ask for and give directions			
5 buy tickets and presents			
6 ask questions using verbs			

1 Find ten words for clothes in the grid. They can be across, down or diagonal.

Ballerinas
Bluse
Hemd
Jeans
Kleid
Lederjacke
Pullover
Sportschuhe
Stiefel
T-Shirt

J	L	B	A	L	L	E	R	I	N	A	S
H	E	M	D	D	I	F	B	S	M	E	P
U	D	A	B	E	S	T	O	K	I	F	O
L	E	O	N	W	Z	H	M	A	G	G	R
L	R	V	D	S	P	A	N	T	K	H	T
A	J	E	K	E	G	N	V	S	Z	P	S
Z	A	R	T	S	H	I	R	T	R	O	C
S	C	U	S	C	H	D	T	I	S	R	H
O	K	P	U	L	L	O	V	E	R	T	U
S	E	D	L	P	Z	N	Z	F	T	V	H
C	K	H	J	B	L	U	S	E	G	W	E
K	E	N	B	U	D	E	K	L	E	I	D

2 🎧 Listen to the adjectives and write in the letter of each one by the appropriate picture.

1 ☐   2 €500 ☐   3 €5 ☐   4 ☐

5 a   6 ☐   7 ☐   8 ☐

3 Choose *ist* or *sind*.

a Der Pullover (ist) / sind zu klein.

b Die Jeans ist / sind schick.

c Die Stiefel ist / sind teuer.

d Die Shorts ist / sind hässlich.

e Der Mantel ist / sind zu lang.

f Die Sportschuhe ist / sind unbequem.

1 Read the article and work out who is who. Write the names in the blanks.

Aischa

SUPER-GIRLS

Wir präsentieren die 'Super-Girls', eine tolle neue Band aus Augsburg. **Jennifer** trägt einen weißen Kapuzenpullover und blaue Shorts. **Maike** trägt eine coole Hose und eine modische Jacke. **Aischa** trägt eine schwarze Jeans und ein rotes T-Shirt. **Fatima** trägt einen schönen Rock und eine gelbe Bluse.

2 Read the article again and fill in the gaps in English.

a Jennifer's hoody is _____white_____ and her shorts are _____ .

b Maike's trousers are _____ and her jacket is _____ .

c Aischa's jeans are _____ and her T-shirt is _____ .

d Fatima's skirt is _____ and her blouse is _____ .

| blue | yellow | black | white | red | nice | fashionable | cool |

3 Write in the correct endings.

a Ich möchte ein<u>en</u> lässig<u>en</u> Rock kaufen.

b Ich möchte ein___ bequem___ Jeans tragen.

c Ich möchte ein___ billig___ Hemd kaufen.

d Ich möchte ein___ modisch___ Jacke haben.

e Ich möchte ein___ rot___ Pullover tragen.

masculine	feminine	neuter
einen …en	eine …e	ein …es

masculine	feminine	neuter
Rock	Jeans	Hemd
Pullover	Jacke	

4A.3 Wir gehen einkaufen!

1 🎧 **Listen to the conversation. Write numbers to show the order in which the items are mentioned. If the item isn't mentioned, leave it blank.**

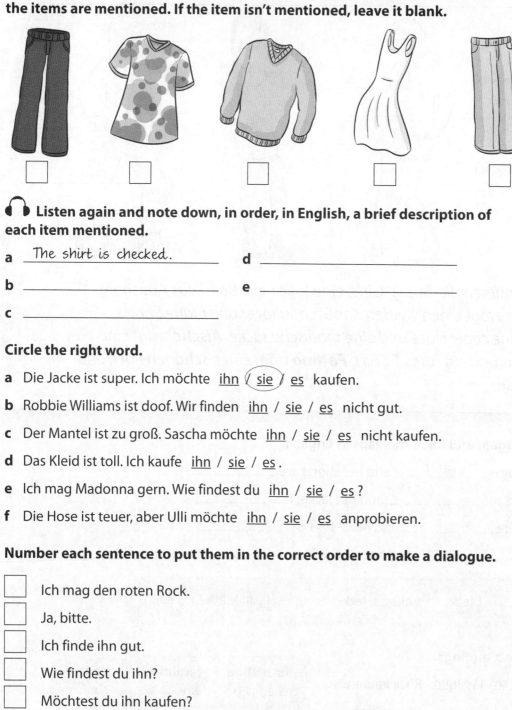

☐ ☐ ☐ ☐ ☐ 1

2 🎧 **Listen again and note down, in order, in English, a brief description of each item mentioned.**

a The shirt is checked.

b _____

c _____

d _____

e _____

3 **Circle the right word.**

a Die Jacke ist super. Ich möchte ihn / (sie) / es kaufen.

b Robbie Williams ist doof. Wir finden ihn / sie / es nicht gut.

c Der Mantel ist zu groß. Sascha möchte ihn / sie / es nicht kaufen.

d Das Kleid ist toll. Ich kaufe ihn / sie / es .

e Ich mag Madonna gern. Wie findest du ihn / sie / es ?

f Die Hose ist teuer, aber Ulli möchte ihn / sie / es anprobieren.

4 **Number each sentence to put them in the correct order to make a dialogue.**

☐ Ich mag den roten Rock.

☐ Ja, bitte.

☐ Ich finde ihn gut.

☐ Wie findest du ihn?

☐ Möchtest du ihn kaufen?

1 Kann ich dir helfen?

☐ Ja, ich kaufe ihn.

☐ Möchtest du ihn anprobieren?

1 **Write in the comparative adjectives in these sentences.**

a Die Stiefel sind ___teurer___ als die Schuhe.

Die Schuhe sind _____ als die Stiefel.

b Der Elefant ist _____ als die Maus.

Die Maus ist _____ als der Elefant.

c Das Auto ist _____ als das Motorrad.

Das Motorrad ist _____ als das Auto.

d Das Monster ist _____ als die Königin.

Die Königin ist _____ als das Monster.

größer	schöner	billiger	kleiner
teurer	neuer	hässlicher	älter

2 **Fill in the gaps to make these sentences future.**

a Ich fahre nach Berlin.

Ich ___werde___ nach Berlin ___fahren___ .

b Wir gehen zu H&M.

Wir _____ zu H&M _____ .

c Ali kauft eine Jeans.

Ali _____ eine Jeans _____ .

d Wir essen Pommes.

Wir _____ Pommes _____ .

e Ich spiele Tischtennis.

Ich _____ Tischtennis _____ .

3 🎧 **Listen to each sentence. Write 'P' if it is present and 'F' if it is future.**

a ☐ P **b** ☐ **c** ☐ **d** ☐ **e** ☐ **f** ☐

1 **Draw lines to link the German and English words.**

interessanter	nice
alt	boring
schön	more boring
schöner	cheaper
älter	uglier
billiger	nicer
billig	more interesting
moderner	cheap
langweilig	more modern
hässlicher	interesting
modern	old
langweiliger	modern
hässlich	ugly
interessant	older

hässlich

alt

2 **Read the text and answer the questions.**

> Wir werden am Samstag in die Stadt gehen und einkaufen. Ich werde einen schönen Pulli und eine schwarze Jeans kaufen. Ich werde zu H&M gehen. Ich finde, H&M ist billiger als Esprit, und auch besser. Meine Kleidung ist nicht mehr modisch. Ich möchte eine lässige Hose und eine schicke Jacke kaufen, aber modische Kleidung ist teuer.

a When is Tanja going shopping?

   On Saturday.

b What's she going to buy? (2 things)

   _____

c Why does she prefer H&M to Esprit? (2 reasons)

   _____

d What else would she like to buy? (2 things)

   _____

e What's the problem?

   _____

Direct object pronouns

1   **Circle the correct word.**

a Ich mag (ihn) / sie / es . (der Pullover)

b Wir finden ihn / sie / es schön. (das Hemd)

c Ich trage ihn / sie / es gern. (die Schuluniform)

d Claudia möchte ihn / sie / es kaufen. (der Rock)

e Ich finde ihn / sie / es zu teuer. (der Computer)

f Mehmet mag ihn / sie / es gern. (das Skateboard)

g Ich möchte ihn / sie / es anprobieren. (die Jeans)

h Wir essen ihn / sie / es nicht gern. (das Fleisch)

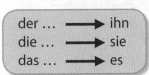

der ... ⟶ ihn
die ... ⟶ sie
das ... ⟶ es

Adjective endings

2   **Write in the correct endings.**

Manja kauft einen gelb_en_ Mantel,

eine modisch____ Jacke,

ein lässig____ T-Shirt, einen warm____ Pullover

und billig____ Schuhe.

masculine	feminine	neuter	plural
einen ...en	eine ...e	ein ...es	...e

masculine	feminine	neuter	plural
Mantel	Jacke	T-Shirt	Schuhe
Pullover			

Manjas Einkaufsliste

Mantel (gelb)

Jacke (modisch)

T-Shirt (lässig)

Pullover (warm)

Schuhe (billig)

werden

3   **Draw lines to link the forms of the verb *werden*.**

ich	sie	du
wirst	wir	werdet
wird	werden	er
ihr	werde	werden

4A.6ᴮ Think

False friends

1 These words look English but each has a different meaning in German. What are the meanings?

> It's surprising the number of German words which look like English ones but mean something completely different. Don't be deceived!

German word   **English meaning**

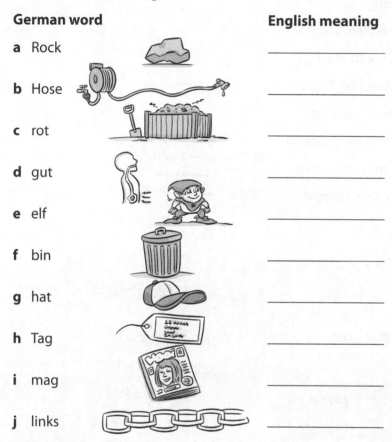

a Rock   _____

b Hose   _____

c rot   _____

d gut   _____

e elf   _____

f bin   _____

g hat   _____

h Tag   _____

i mag   _____

j links   _____

Pronunciation

2 Although the English and German words look the same, they sound different. Read the words in Activity 1 aloud twice, once using the English pronunciation and once using the German.

'Cognates'

3 Look carefully at these words and write C (Cognate) or NC (Near Cognate) by each word.

☐ Pullover   ☐ Musik   ☐ braun

☐ Jeans   ☐ cool   ☐ Spanisch

☐ T-Shirt   ☐ intelligent   ☐ Mathe

☐ Bluse   ☐ Elefant   ☐ Sport

☐ Party   ☐ Banane   ☐ Gitarre

> In contrast to 'false friends', 'cognate' words are words which look and mean the same in English and German. 'Near cognates' mean the same but are spelled slightly differently.

Die Jeans ist cool! — *Jeans are cool!*

die Ballerinas	*pumps/ballerina shoes*
die Bluse	*blouse*
das Hemd	*shirt*
die Hose	*trousers*
die Jeans	*jeans*
der Kapuzenpullover	*hoodie*
das Kleid	*dress*
die Kleidung	*clothes/clothing*
die Lederjacke	*leather jacket*
der Mantel	*coat*
der Pullover	*jumper*
der Rock	*skirt*
die Shorts	*shorts*
die Sportschuhe	*trainers*
die Stiefel	*boots*
das T-Shirt	*T-shirt*

alt	*old*
altmodisch	*old-fashioned*
bequem	*comfortable*
billig	*cheap*
bunt	*multicoloured*
gestreift	*stripy*
hässlich	*ugly*
kariert	*checked*
kurz	*short*
lässig	*casual*
modisch	*fashionable*
neu	*new*
schick	*chic/smart*
schön	*beautiful*
teuer	*expensive*
unbequem	*uncomfortable*

sehr	*very*
total	*totally*
ziemlich	*quite*

Coole Outfits — *Cool outfits*

Ich trage …	*I wear …*
Er/Sie trägt …	*He/She wears …*
… einen gelben Rock	*… a yellow skirt*
… ein teures Kleid	*… an expensive dress*
… eine schwarze Jacke	*… a black jacket*
… lässige Shorts	*… casual shorts*
normalerweise	*normally/usually*
Ich möchte … tragen.	*I'd like to wear …*
Ich möchte … kaufen.	*I'd like to buy …*
Ich möchte einkaufen gehen.	*I'd like to go shopping.*
Ich möchte schick aussehen.	*I'd like to look smart.*

Wir gehen einkaufen! — *We're going shopping!*

Wie findest du …?	*What do you think of …?*
Ich finde ihn/sie/es …	*I find it …*

Ich finde sie (pl) …	*I find them …*
zu groß/klein	*too big/small*
zu teuer	*too expensive*
Es steht dir gut.	*It suits you.*
Es steht dir nicht.	*It doesn't suit you.*
Wie kann ich dir helfen?	*How can I help you?*
Ich möchte (ihn) anprobieren.	*I'd like to try it on.*
Ich möchte (sie) kaufen.	*I'd like to buy it/them.*
Ich möchte (es) nicht kaufen.	*I wouldn't like to buy it.*

Die Hose ist zu klein! — *The trousers are too small!*

Mein Outfit ist zu alt.	*My outfit is too old.*
Ich werde einkaufen gehen.	*I'll go shopping.*
Ich werde … kaufen.	*I'll buy …*
Ich werde (ihn) umtauschen.	*I'll exchange it.*
Ich werde … tragen.	*I'll wear …*
eine Größe kleiner	*a size smaller*
eine Größe größer	*a size bigger*
besser (als)	*better (than)*

Das trage ich! — *That's what I wear!*

Was trägst du gern?	*What do you like wearing?*
Ich trage (am liebsten) …	*My favourite clothes are …*
Wo kaufst du ein?	*Where do you go shopping?*
Ich kaufe meine Kleidung bei …	*I buy my clothes at …*
Was trägst du in der Schule?	*What do you wear at school?*
In der Schule trage ich …	*At school I wear …*
die Schuluniform	*school uniform*
die Designerkleidung	*designer clothing*
die Krawatte	*tie*
hellblau	*light blue*

Checklist

How well do you think you can do the following?			
Write a sentence for each one if you can.			
	I can do this well	**I can do this but not very well**	**I can't do this yet**
1 talk about, compare and give opinions on clothes			
2 use the singular and plural forms of nouns followed by *ist* and *sind*			
3 use adjective endings in the accusative case			
4 use *ich möchte* correctly			
5 use the words for 'it' (*ihn/sie/es*) and 'them' (*sie*)			
6 use the future tense			

4B.1 Die Ferien

1 🎧 **Listen to the conversation and circle the right information.**

a Olaf is going to   Italy / (Spain) / Turkey .

b He is going by   train / plane / car .

c He will stay in a   hotel / caravan / apartment .

d He's staying for   a week / two weeks / a month .

e The weather there is   always / sometimes / never   sunny.

f He's going   on his own / with other people .

2 **Choose *einer* or *einem*.**

a Ich wohne in (einem) / einer   Wohnwagen.

b Wir wohnen in einem / einer   Jugendherberge.

c Ich wohne auf einem / einer   Campingplatz.

d Jessica wohnt in einem / einer   Wohnmobil.

e Mohammad wohnt in einem / einer   Ferienwohnung.

f Ich wohne in einem / einer   Ferienhaus.

masculine	feminine	neuter
in einem	einer	einem

masculine	feminine	neuter
Wohnwagen	Jugendherberge	Wohnmobil
Campingplatz	Ferienwohnung	Ferienhaus

3 **Fill in the grid in English.**

	Mode of transport	Where?
a	car	
b		
c		
d		

a Wir fahren mit dem Auto nach Italien.

b Ich fahre mit dem Zug nach Österreich.

c Ursel fliegt in die Türkei.

d Familie Müller fährt mit dem Wohnmobil nach Frankreich.

1 Complete the sentences in the same order as the places are mentioned in the brochure.

Hansestadt Hamburg

In Hamburg gibt es …

➡ *einen Hafen*

➡ *einen Marktplatz*

➡ *viele Fischrestaurants*

➡ *einen Zoo (Hagenbecks Tierpark)*

➡ *den Dom (Freizeitpark)*

➡ *ein Schifffahrtsmuseum*

a Wir können ___eine Hafenrundfahrt machen.___

b Wir können _____

c Wir können _____.

d Wir können _____.

e Wir können _____.

f Wir können _____.

> The *Dom* in Hamburg isn't a cathedral (the usual meaning of the word); it's a huge fairground.
> You can work out the meaning of *Schifffahrtsmuseum* because it's made up of words you will recognise.

> Fisch essen   ins Museum gehen
> eine Hafenrundfahrt machen   Karussell fahren
> zum Zoo gehen   auf dem Markt einkaufen

2 🎧 Listen to these people planning a day out in Hamburg. Put a tick by the things they plan to do and a cross by those they don't.

They are going to …

a ✔ go to the zoo.

b ☐ do a harbour tour.

c ☐ go shopping in a big store.

d ☐ go shopping at the market.

e ☐ eat fish.

f ☐ visit a museum.

g ☐ go to the fairground.

1 🎧 **Listen to these people talking.**
Circle Past, Present or Future.

a Past / Present / (Future)

b Past / Present / Future

c Past / Present / Future

d Past / Present / Future

e Past / Present / Future

f Past / Present / Future

g Past / Present / Future

h Past / Present / Future

2 **Circle the correct form.**

a Wir (haben) / sind Tennis gespielt.

b Ich habe / bin nach Spanien gefahren.

c Wir haben / sind nach Frankfurt geflogen.

d Ich habe / bin in einem Hotel gewohnt.

e Wir haben / sind mit dem Zug gefahren.

f Wir haben / sind einen Ausflug gemacht.

> *fahren* and *fliegen* use
> *sein* in the perfect tense.

3 **Complete the sentences with the correct past participle.**

a 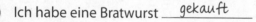 Ich habe eine Bratwurst ___gekauft___ .

b Wir haben Tennis _____ .

c Wir haben eine Stadtrundfahrt _____ .

d 🎵 Ich habe Musik _____ .

> gemacht   gehört   gekauft   gespielt

4B.4 Im Prater

1 Write in the correct words.

a Wir haben ____letztes____ ____Wochenende____ einen Ausflug nach Wien gemacht.

(*last weekend*)

b Ich werde _____ in der Disco tanzen. (*tomorrow*)

c Wir spielen _____ mit dem Computer. (*today*)

d Ich esse _____ _____ Cornflakes. (*every day*)

e Angela geht _____ _____ _____ schwimmen. (*twice a week*)

f Boris ist _____ ins Kino gegangen. (*yesterday*)

> gestern   heute   morgen   jeden Tag
> zweimal in der Woche   letztes Wochenende

2 🎧 Listen to the phone conversation and circle Past, Present or Future.

a travelling by underground train   <u>Past</u> / Present / Future

b playing cards   Past / Present / Future

c going on fairground rides   Past / Present / Future

d going to the cinema   Past / Present / Future

e listening to music   Past / Present / Future

f staying in   Past / Present / Future

1 🎧 **Listen to these people talking about holidays and write in the information in English.**

a Already done: _gone to England_

Will do: _____

b Already done: _____

Will do: _____

c Already done: _____

Will do: _____

d Already done: _____

Will do: _____

2 **Read the sentences and write F (*falsch* = wrong) or R (*richtig* = right).**

> Ich bin letzte Woche mit meiner Familie nach München gefahren. München ist eine tolle Stadt. Wir haben eine Stadtrundfahrt gemacht und ich habe ein neues T-Shirt gekauft. In München kann man gut essen und trinken. Das Bier ist billig, aber ich bin noch zu jung für Bier. Nächste Woche werden wir nach Innsbruck fahren. Das ist in Österreich. Wir werden Ski laufen und Snowboard fahren. Das Wetter in Österreich ist kalt im Winter.

Joachim

a [F] Joachim is going to Munich next week.

b [ ] He's going alone.

c [ ] Munich is great.

d [ ] He did a tour of the city.

e [ ] He bought a T-Shirt.

f [ ] He drank beer.

g [ ] He went to Innsbruck last week as well.

h [ ] Innsbruck is in Switzerland.

i [ ] He will go skiing.

j [ ] It will be hot in Innsbruck.

Perfect tense with *haben* or *sein*

1 Circle the correct form of *haben* or *sein*.

a Wir habe / (haben) Eis gegessen.

b Ich habe / haben eine Jacke gekauft.

c Wir habe / haben in einem Hotel gewohnt.

d Ich habe / haben Gitarre gespielt.

e Wir bin / sind in die Schule gegangen.

f Ich bin / sind nach Italien gefahren.

g Wir bin / sind nach Amerika geflogen.

h Ich bin / sind zum Imbiss gegangen.

> Ich habe / bin …   + past participle
> Wir haben / sind …   at the end.

2 Fill in the gaps. Look back through this unit to find the information.

verb	past participle	*haben* or *sein*?
machen	gemacht	haben
hören	_____	_____
fahren	_____	_____
tanzen	_____	_____
gehen	_____	_____
essen	_____	_____
fliegen	_____	_____
kaufen	_____	_____
wohnen	_____	_____

einem / einer

3 Fill in the gaps with *einem* or *einer*.

a auf _____ Campingplatz

b in _____ Hotel

c in _____ Jugendherberge

d in _____ Ferienwohnung

e in _____ Wohnwagen

f in _____ Gasthaus

> Not heard the word *Gasthaus* before? No problem. It's very similar to an English word, so you can work out the meaning. And you know its gender, so you can work out the dative. That's why German is so easy!

masculine	feminine	neuter
Campingplatz	Jugendherberge	Hotel
Wohnwagen	Ferienwohnung	Gasthaus

masculine	feminine	neuter
einem	einer	einem

Compound nouns

1 Find compound nouns meaning:

a a hostel for youth   Jugendherberge

b a house for holidays   _____

c a place for camping   _____

d a car for living in   _____

e a park for free time   _____

f a journey round a town   _____

g a bath for swimming   _____

h a huge wheel   _____

i a cupboard for clothes   _____

j ice made with chocolate   _____

Schokoladeneis

Freizeitpark

Riesenrad

Stadtrundfahrt

Ferienhaus

Wohnwagen

Kleiderschrank

Jugendherberge

Schwimmbad

Campingplatz

It's fun to analyse the structure of words in German because so many words are constructed from putting together other words to make a new meaning. It also helps you to understand words which may seem new but are actually made out of words you already know.

Opinions

2 Write P (positive) or N (negative) next to these opinions.

a [P] Ich freue mich darauf.

b [ ] Das finde ich langweilig.

c [ ] Das finde ich nicht langweilig.

d [ ] Das ist toll.

e [ ] Ich freue mich nicht darauf.

f [ ] Das gefällt mir.

g [ ] Das macht Spaß!

h [ ] Das gefällt mir nicht.

Expressing your opinions is important and it can also help you to reach a higher National Curriculum level in German. Examples of ways to give opinions are:
- using positive and negative adjectives
- *Ich finde …* (I think / find …)
- *Ich freue mich …* (I'm looking forward …)
- *Das gefällt mir.* (It pleases me / I like it.)

Here are some listening skills to take on to the next part of the course.
- Get clues from pictures and titles.
- Read the questions carefully.
- Anticipate probable answers and see if you are right.
- Listen to the tone of voice for clues.

Wohin fährst du in den Ferien?	*Where are you going on holiday?*
Ich fahre/Wir fahren …	*I am/We are going …*
nach Frankreich	*to France*
nach Italien	*to Italy*
an die Nordsee	*to the North Sea*
in die Türkei	*to Turkey*

Wie fährst du?	*How are you travelling/ going?*
Ich fahre/Wir fahren mit …	*I am/We are going by …*
dem Auto	*car*
dem Wohnmobil	*camper van*
dem Wohnwagen	*caravan*
dem Zug	*train*
Ich fliege/Wir fliegen.	*I am/We are going by plane. I am/We are flying.*

Wo wohnst du?	*Where are you staying?*
Ich wohne/Wir wohnen …	*I am/We are staying …*
auf einem Campingplatz	*on a campsite*
in einem Ferienhaus	*in a holiday home*
in einer Ferienwohnung	*in a holiday apartment*
in einem Hotel	*in a hotel*
in einer Jugendherberge	*in a youth hostel*
in einem Wohnmobil	*in a camper van*
in einem Wohnwagen	*in a caravan*
in einem Zelt	*in a tent*
Wie lange bleibst du/bleibt ihr dort?	*How long are you staying there?*
Ich bleibe/Wir bleiben (eine Woche) dort.	*I am/We are staying there (a week).*
zwei Wochen (lang)	*two weeks*
eine Woche	*one week*
zehn Tage	*ten days*

Was können wir machen?	*What can we do?*
Wir können/wollen …	*We can/want to …*
Ich kann/will …	*I can/want to …*
in einen Freizeitpark gehen	*go to an amusement park*
ins Museum gehen	*go to a museum*
mit dem Riesenrad fahren	*go on the Ferris wheel*
den Stephansdom besuchen	*visit St Stephan's Cathedral*
eine Stadtrundfahrt machen	*go on a tour of the town*
im Wasserpark spielen	*play in the waterpark*
ein Wiener Schnitzel essen	*eat a veal escalope*

Was werdet ihr machen?	*What will you do?*
Wir werden …	*We will …*
(meine) Freunde treffen	*meet up with (my) friends*
ein Eis kaufen	*buy an ice cream*
ein Picknick machen	*go on a picnic*
Pizza essen	*eat pizza*
das Schloss Schönbrunn besuchen	*visit Schönbrunn Palace*
schwimmen	*go swimming*
Souvenirs kaufen	*buy souvenirs*
ins Theater gehen	*go to the theatre*

Was hast du gemacht?	*What did you do?*
Wir haben/Ich habe …	*We/I …*
einen Ausflug gemacht	*went on an excursion*
in der Disco getanzt	*danced in the disco*
Frisbee gespielt	*played frisbee*
Karten gekauft	*bought tickets*
Musik im Park gehört	*listened to music in the park*
Souvenirs gekauft	*bought souvenirs*

Wohin bist du gefahren?	*Where did you go?*
Ich bin/Wir sind …	*I/We …*
nach Italien gefahren	*went to Italy*
in die Türkei geflogen	*flew to Turkey*
Wo hast du gewohnt?	*Where did you stay?*
Ich habe/Wir haben in … gewohnt.	*I/We stayed in …*

Checklist

How well do you think you can do the following? Write a sentence for each one if you can.	I can do this well	I can do this but not very well	I can't do this yet
1 say where you are going on holiday			
2 say how you are getting there			
3 say where you are staying and for how long			
4 describe a holiday in the past			
5 use modal verbs correctly			
6 use the perfect tense correctly			

Zoom Deutsch 1

Zoom in on your students' needs for KS3 German
with fully integrated video drama

Zoom Deutsch is an inspiring two-part German course offering fresh, exciting material and a fully integrated video drama for the whole ability range at Key Stage 3.

The course is flexible and relevant, taking account of the ever increasing diversity of students' abilities and language learning backgrounds. It is fully up-to-date and follows the renewed Key Stage 3 Framework for Languages and the revised Key Stage 3 Programme of Study.

This Workbook provides:

- differentiated practice material for the key language in each unit
- consolidation of key grammar points and language learning skills
- checklists and vocabulary lists for each unit so students can revise the language they've learnt and check their progress
- extra audio material for listening practice

Zoom Deutsch Student Book 1	978 0 19 912770 2
Zoom Deutsch Foundation Workbook 1	978 0 19 912810 5
Zoom Deutsch Higher Workbook 1	978 0 19 912811 2
Zoom Deutsch Teacher Book 1	978 0 19 912775 7
Zoom Deutsch Audio CDs 1	978 0 19 912773 3
Zoom Deutsch Interactive Oxbox 1	978 0 19 912776 4
Zoom Deutsch Assessment Oxbox 1	978 0 19 912777 1

OXFORD

UNIVERSITY PRESS

How to get in touch:
web www.oxfordsecondary.co.uk
email schools.enquiries.uk@oup.com
tel 01536 452620
fax 01865 313472

ISBN 978-0-19-912771-9

9 780199 127719